DRAWING Spaceships

Don Bolognese

Franklin Watts
London New York Sydney Toronto

To Darren and Carlyn,
space pioneers of the future

First published in the United States of America
by Franklin Watts Inc, New York.
This edition first published in Great Britain 1984 by
Franklin Watts Limited
12a Golden Square
London, W1R 4BA

ISBN 0 86313 117 4

Printed in Great Britain by Garden City Press, Letchworth.

CONTENTS

USA

Introduction

3–2–1! Ignition! Lift-off! The voice from mission control is audible even over the roar of the rocket engines.

This is it—the moment you've waited for eagerly. Your eyes scan the control panel. If anything goes wrong, you have to know it instantly. So far everything looks good.

Up you go, through the thin layer of clouds—higher and higher—until the blue of earth's sky becomes the blackness of space.

Suddenly, there is silence. All the engines have stopped. You are in space. You've trained and planned for this mission for years. You've seen thousands of films—but you never expected this sight. . . .

One day, some of us may actually experience space flight. But until then we will have to rely on our imaginations. We will be able to travel to the stars only through the creativity of writers, the special effects of moviemakers, and the magic of artists—like you.

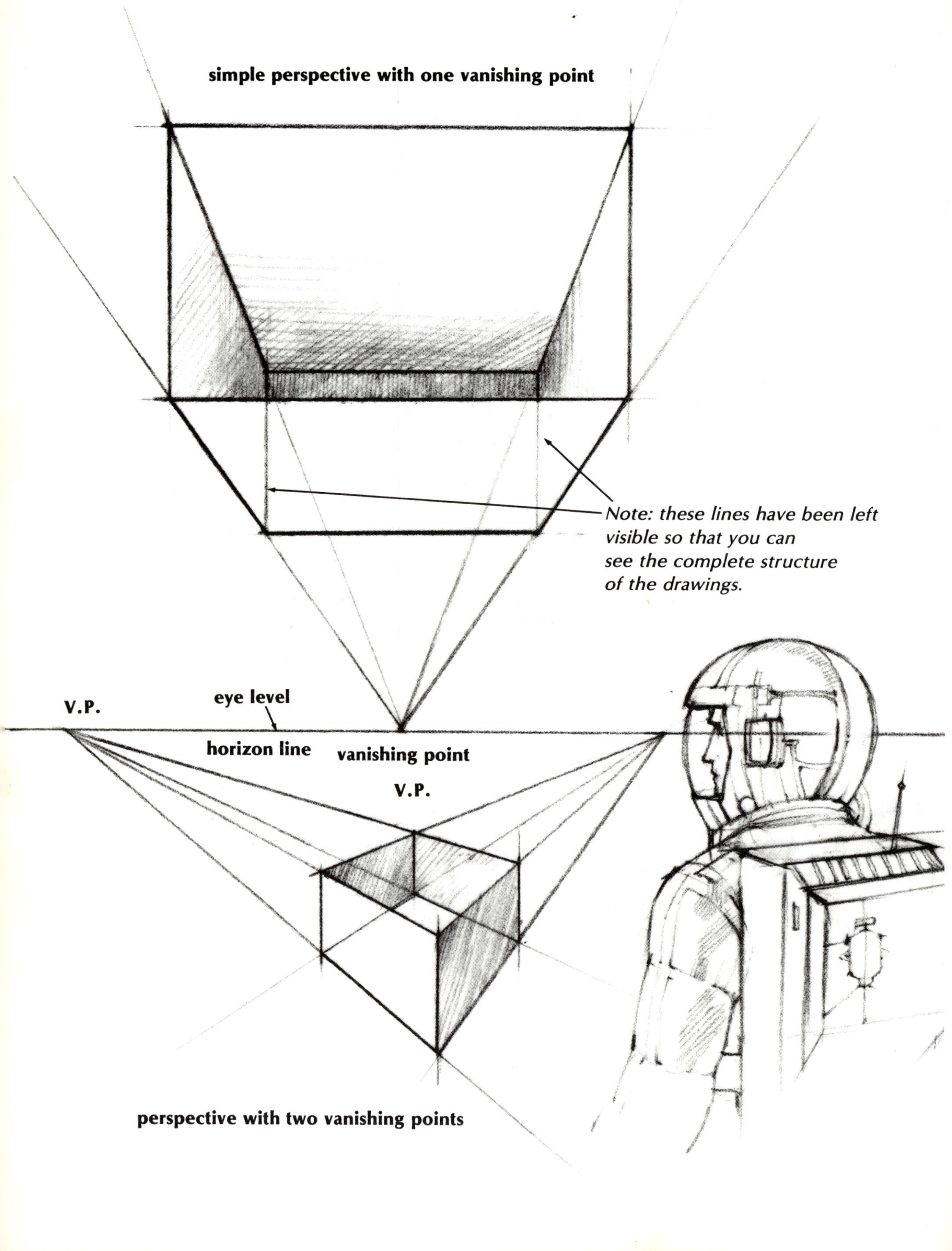
simple perspective with one vanishing point
Note: these lines have been left visible so that you can see the complete structure of the drawings.
V.P.
eye level
horizon line
vanishing point
V.P.
perspective with two vanishing points

CHAPTER 1 Preparing for Space

The biggest difference between drawings set on earth and drawings set in outer space is in the way the artist creates a sense of distance. In space there are no trees or buildings or other familiar shapes to help us know if something is near or far. Space is vast and seems empty. But an artist must still show whether an object is coming toward us or going away.

One very useful tool is perspective. Most of us are familiar with perspective. Perspective is a way of drawing an object so that it appears to go back into the distance. Artists have made use of it for centuries. It is not complicated if you remember a few simple points.

As illustrated on the left, there are two steps to begin. First draw the eye level, or horizon line. Next establish your vanishing points: the points where the parallel lines of an object meet.

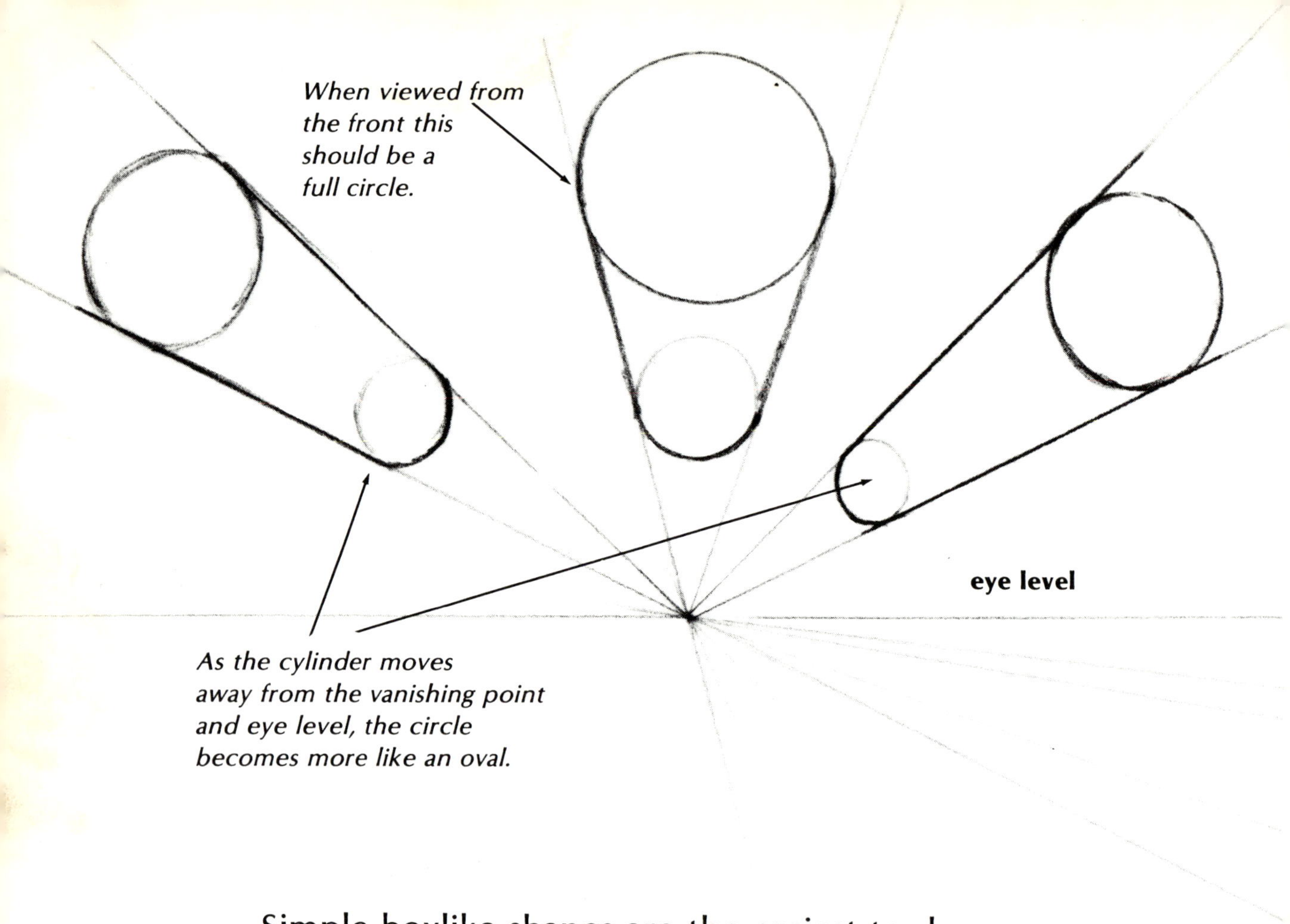

Simple boxlike shapes are the easiest to draw in perspective. All you have to do is make all the lines that go in the same direction meet at the vanishing point. Perspective can also be used in drawing cylindrical objects (see illustration above). Remember that perspective is only an aid to your drawing. If you can achieve a sense of space and distance without it—fine. However, if you are having trouble making a particular form (a spaceship for example) appear convincing, you might want to check its perspective. Refer to these illustrations often as you proceed.

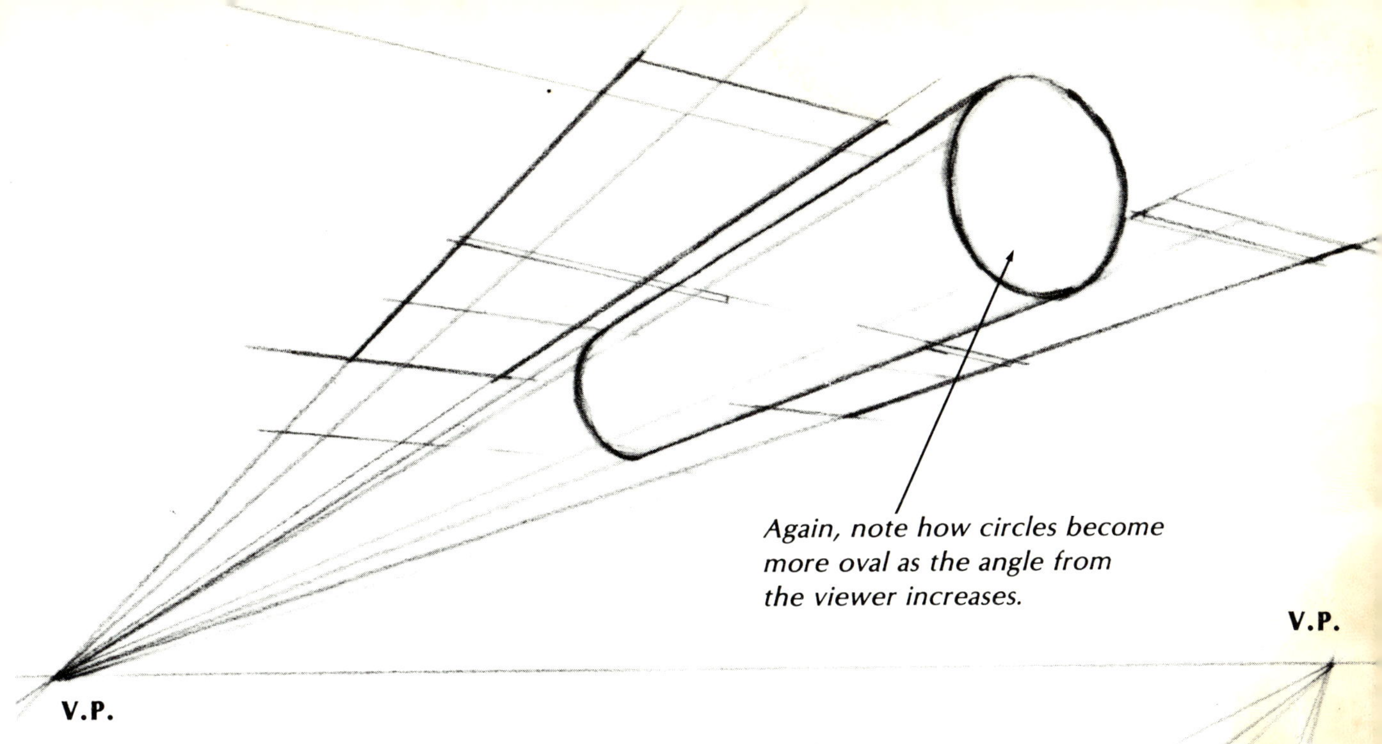

Again, note how circles become more oval as the angle from the viewer increases.

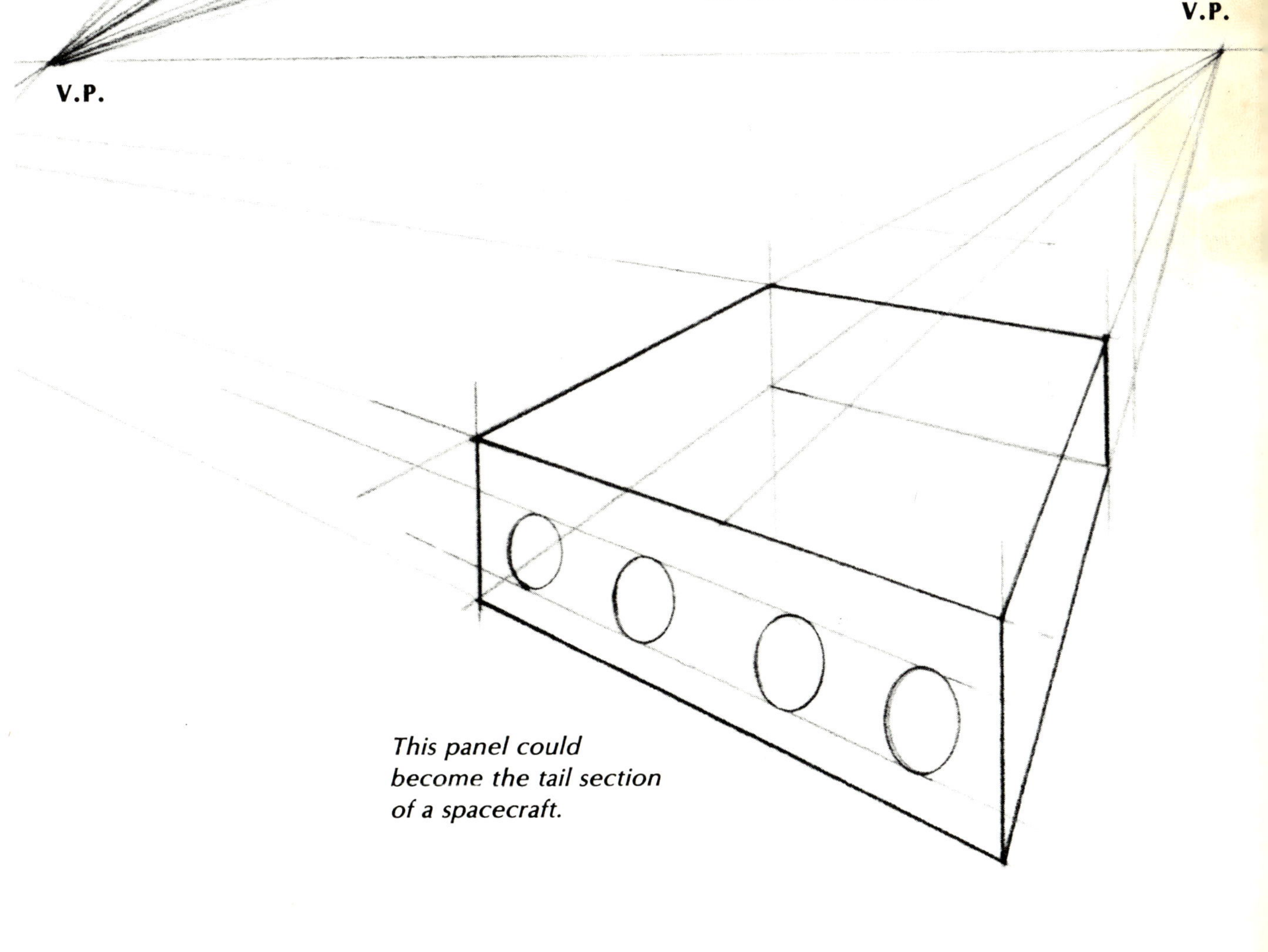

This panel could become the tail section of a spacecraft.

At an actual space centre operated by NASA or at the Air and Space Museum in Washington, D.C., you can see real spacecraft. Most of us, however, can only see these vehicles in books or films or as toy models. There are kits from which you can build scale models of the Space Shuttle and other spacecraft. And there are kits that allow you to design and build your own spaceship.

Of course, the most available reference source is pictures. If you haven't got one already, begin a picture collection. Put your favourite pictures where you can always see them. They will excite your imagination when you begin inventing your own spacecraft designs.

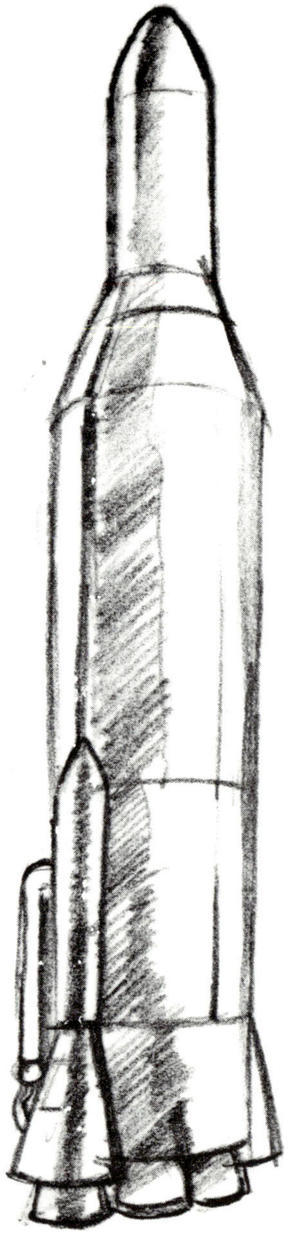

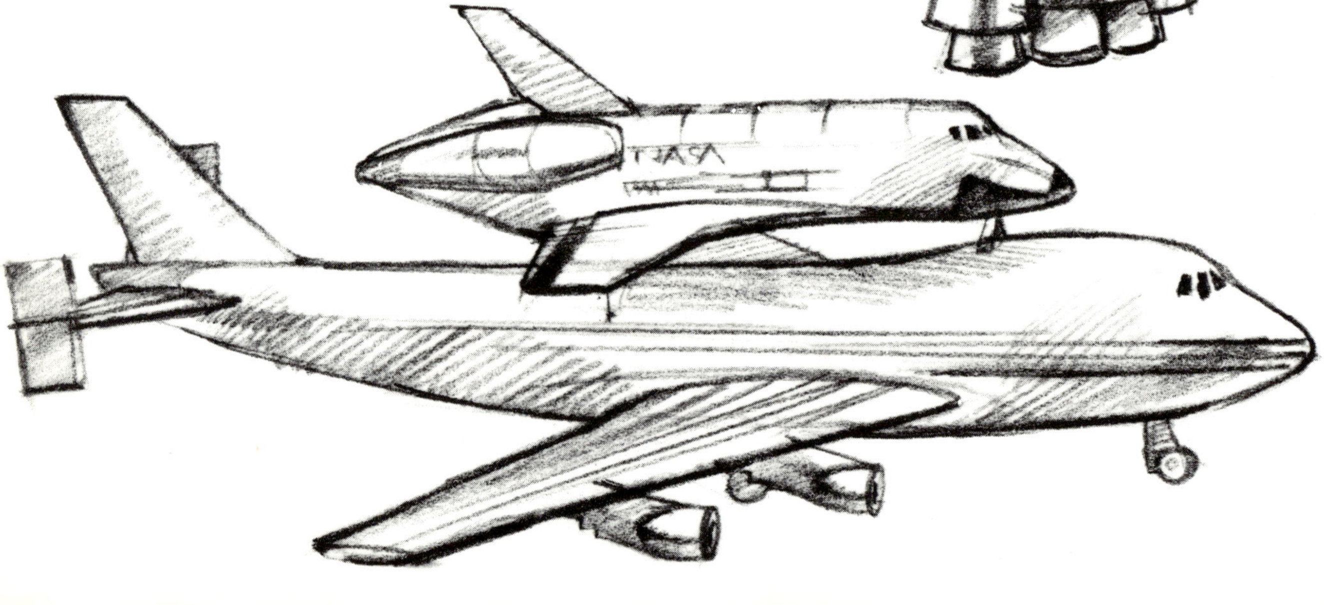

Art Supplies

Pencils—From H (light) to 4B (dark)

Erasers—Kneaded and plastic erasers

Paper—Any good bond paper or tracing paper. For larger, more finished work use illustration board.

Fixative—A matte finish workable fixative for pencil drawings

Lightbox for tracing—Working up your drawing through the sketch phase to a more finished picture can be much easier with a lightbox. The simplest lightbox is a window with light coming through. Tape a drawing to the window. Then tape a fresh paper over the drawing and trace it. If the paper is too thick, the light will not go through it. A simple desktop lightbox can be made by putting pieces of glass (frosted, if possible) in a frame built up enough so that a light bulb can be placed beneath it.

Draughtsman's tools

It is important for a student of drawing to gain confidence, which only comes from constant practice. And that means sketching often and with concentration. The hand and eye will learn to coordinate in order to translate the artist's mental images into real pictures. Almost all artists sketch freehand—in other words, without mechanical aids such as rulers, circular or oval patterns, curves, and compasses. For example, all the preliminary sketches in this book were done freehand. However, spacecraft are precision-made machines. Their forms and details require a degree of exactness if the drawing is to be realistic. That's where these tools come in: *after* you have sketched your rough picture to your satisfaction. Whenever tools are used in this book, they will be identified so that you can understand their use. Remember that you do not absolutely need all the tools shown, but it would be unfair to you not to explain how professional artists achieve some of the realistic effects that you admire.

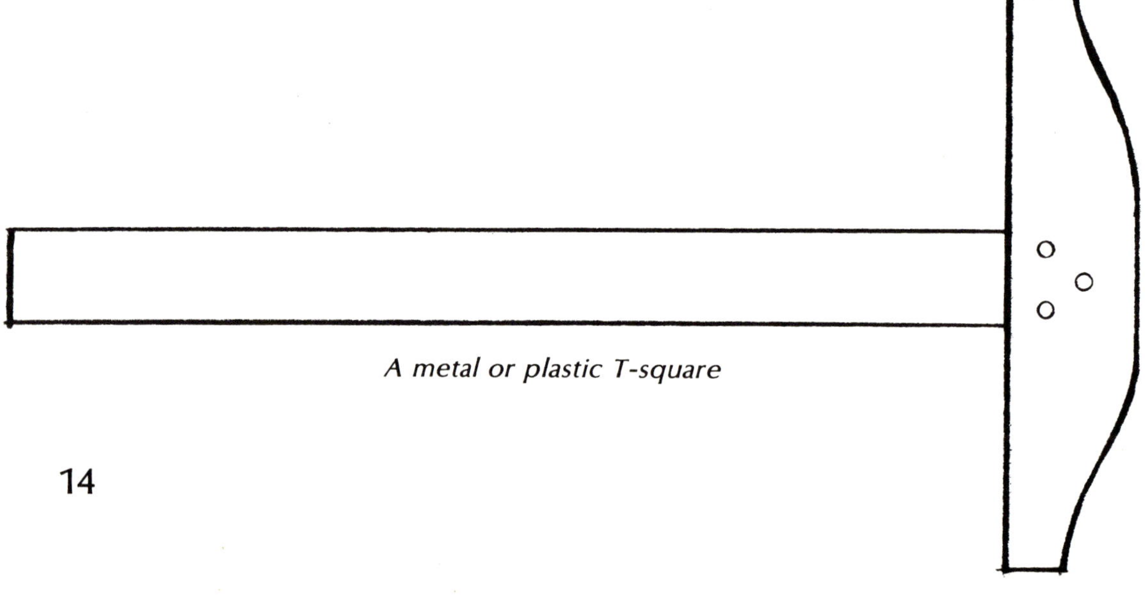

A metal or plastic T-square

Plastic templates come in a variety of circles and ovals.

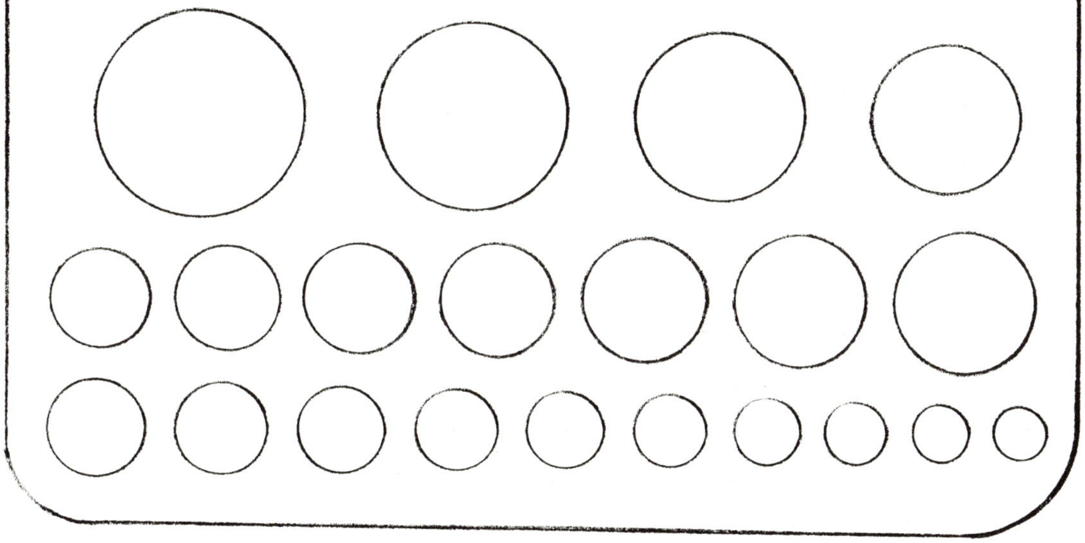

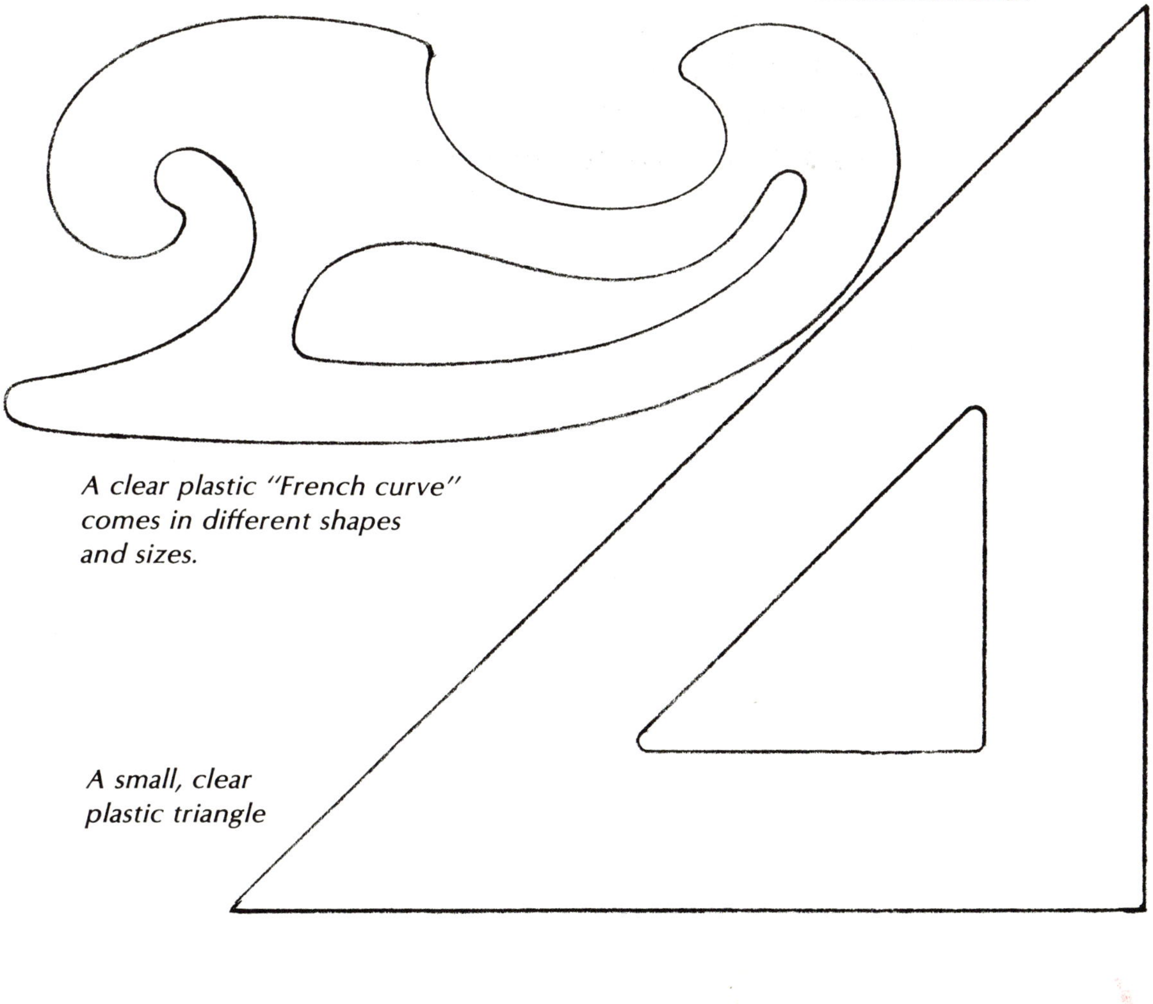

A clear plastic "French curve" comes in different shapes and sizes.

A small, clear plastic triangle

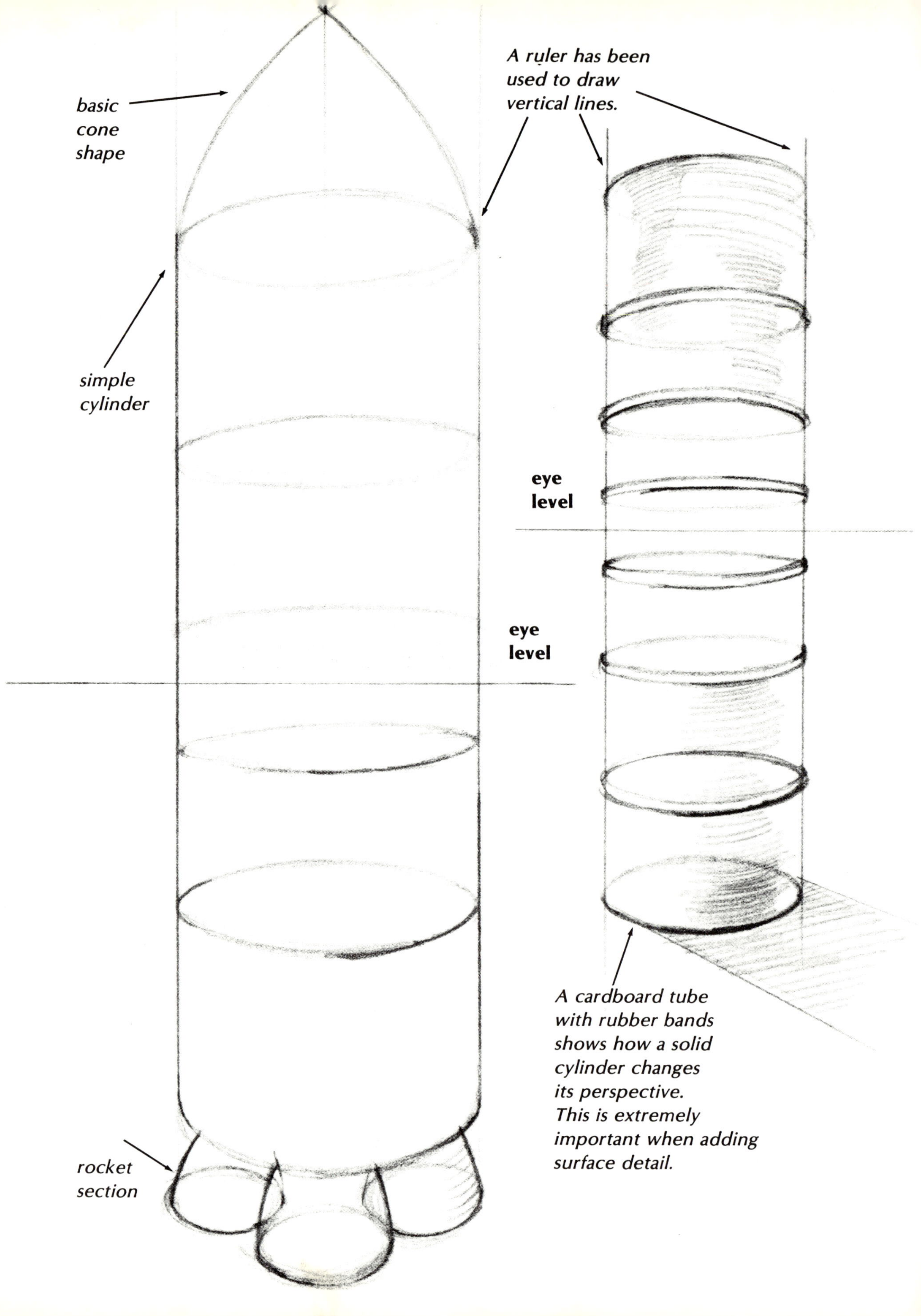
basic cone shape
A ruler has been used to draw vertical lines.
simple cylinder
eye level
eye level
A cardboard tube with rubber bands shows how a solid cylinder changes its perspective. This is extremely important when adding surface detail.
rocket section

CHAPTER 2 Blast-off

The first thing you must do in order to travel in space is to leave earth. This means that your spacecraft has to overcome two basic physical forces: gravity and atmospheric resistance, or the resistance of air. Conquering gravity requires power—huge rocket engines. And overcoming air resistance calls for streamlined, or aerodynamic, design. That is why all of the existing spacecraft are basically simple geometric shapes: a cone, on top of a smooth cylinder, on top of a powerful rocket. Fortunately, we can use ordinary objects such as cardboard tubes (see illustration at left) and paper cups as models. The easy experiments on the next few pages will help you to understand the basic elements of spacecraft design.

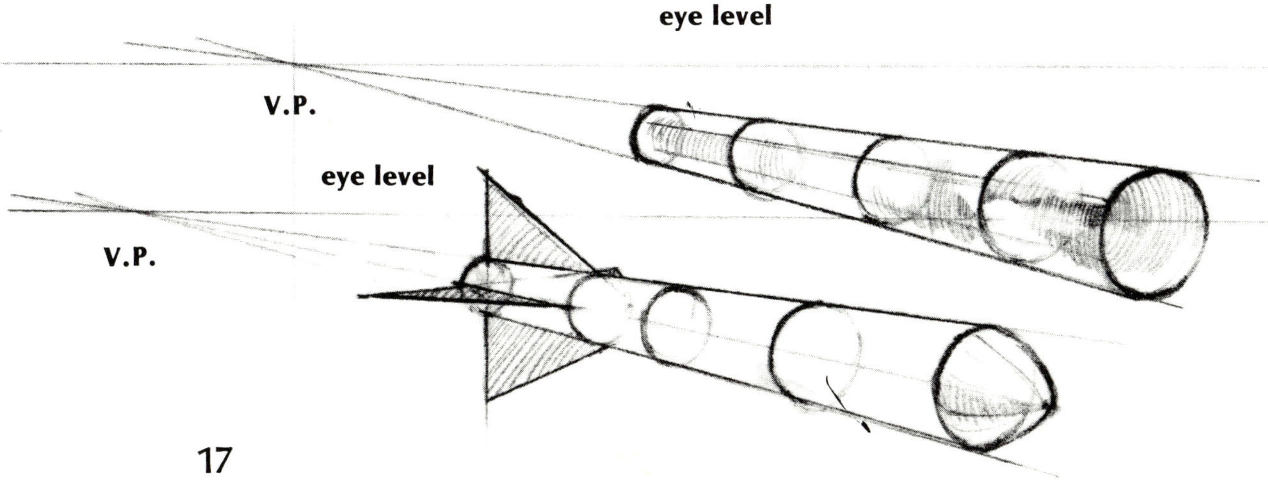

DSOA-2

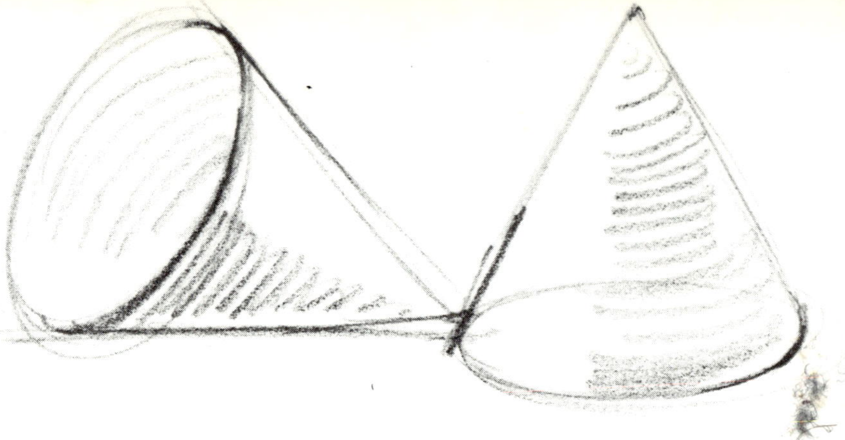

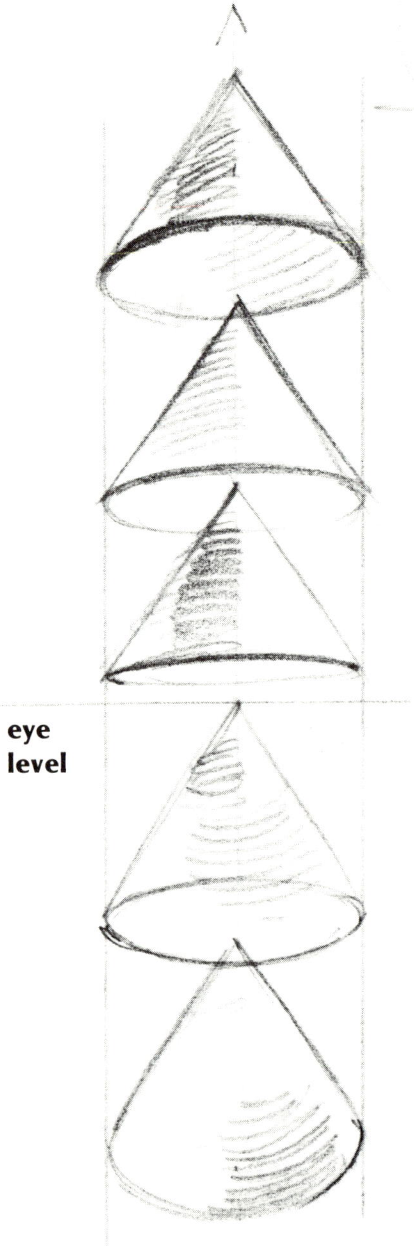

Cones

Because a conelike shape is the basic form for the front end of all rockets, you should try to draw it from as many angles as possible. The series at left shows how perspective is used when drawing the cone shape as you see it above and below eye level.

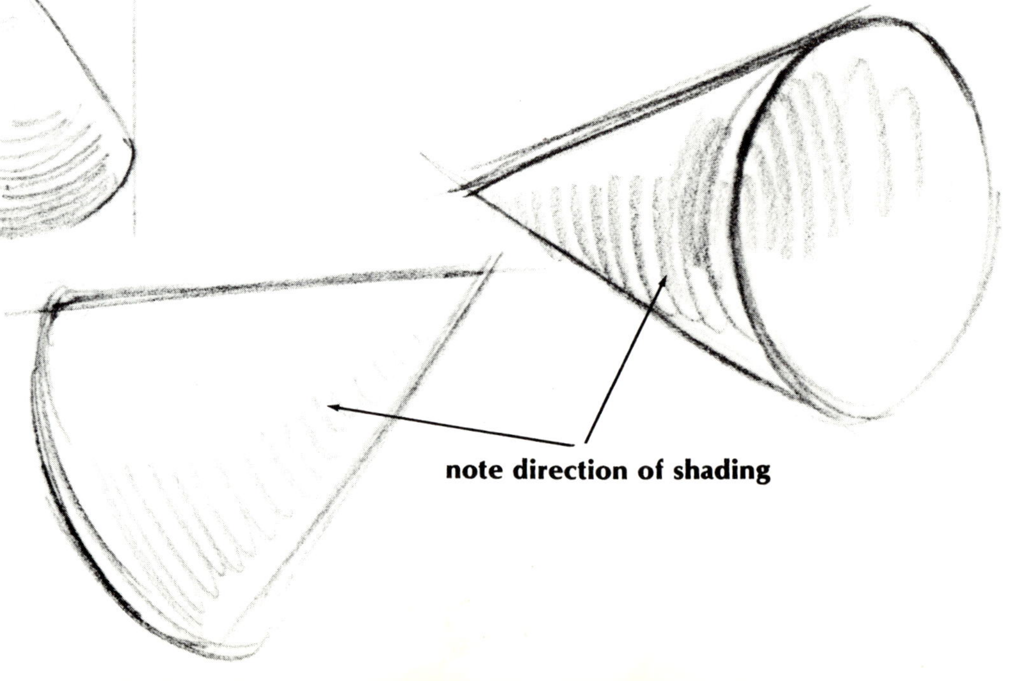

APOLLO

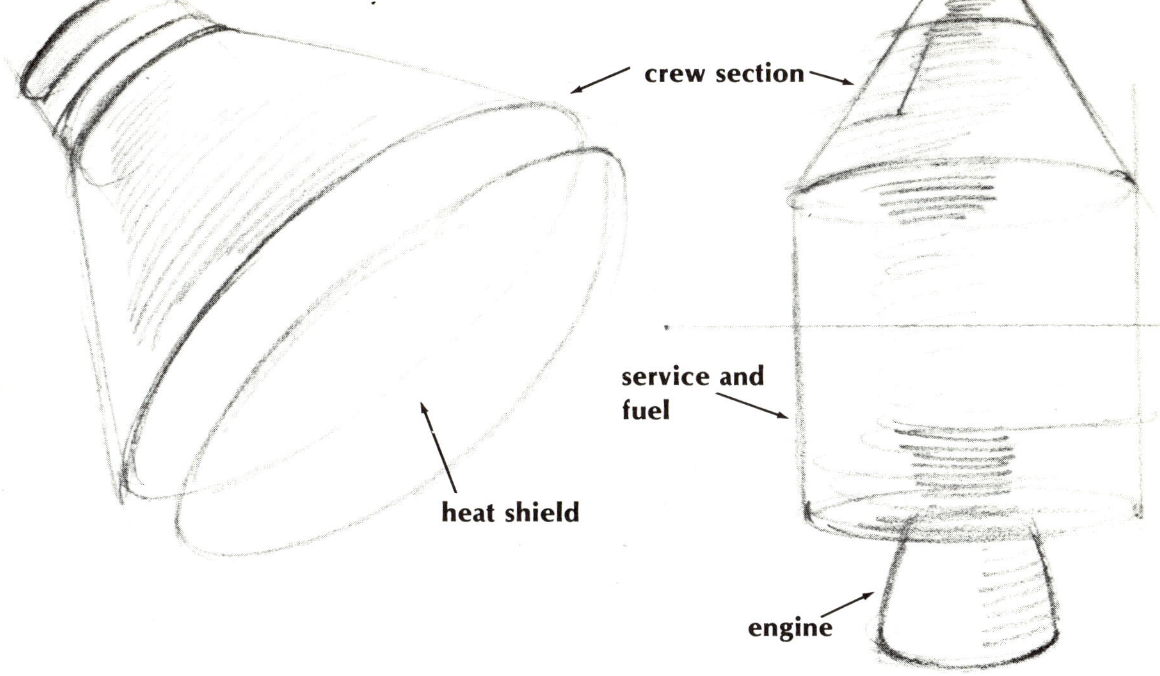

The Apollo capsule shows how the basic cone shape can be suited to spacecraft design.

Another example of the cone shape is used in small manoeuvring rockets. These rockets are used to adjust the spacecraft's position and/or altitude. They are used in delicate operations such as one spacecraft docking with another.

basic shape of small rockets

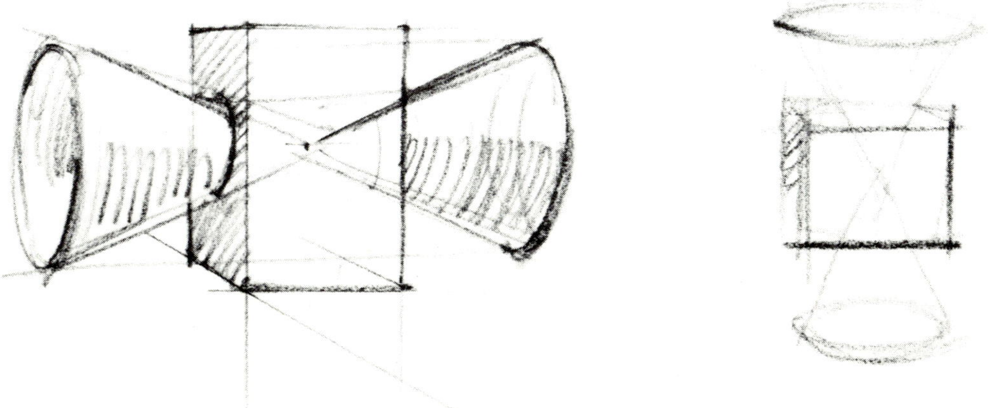

Cones as Rocket Engines

For the fun of it, paste some paper cups on a circular piece of cardboard (top illustration). Hold the cardboard and place it above your eye level. Can you imagine it as the bottom of a huge rocket? Now imagine ignition has just taken place (illustration at right). This simple experiment can be a big help in all your drawings of rocket engines. Knowing how to draw these engines in all positions is one of the keys to drawing realistic spacecraft.

These highlights are achieved by using a kneaded eraser.

Have you noticed that surface details have been ignored in these basic drawings? The details on spacecraft are really fun to draw. But you will see that they will be more convincing if the basic form is well drawn; so for now try hard not to get too distracted by windows, hatches, antennas, insignias, etc. We'll get to them soon.

Fins, Flaps, and Wings

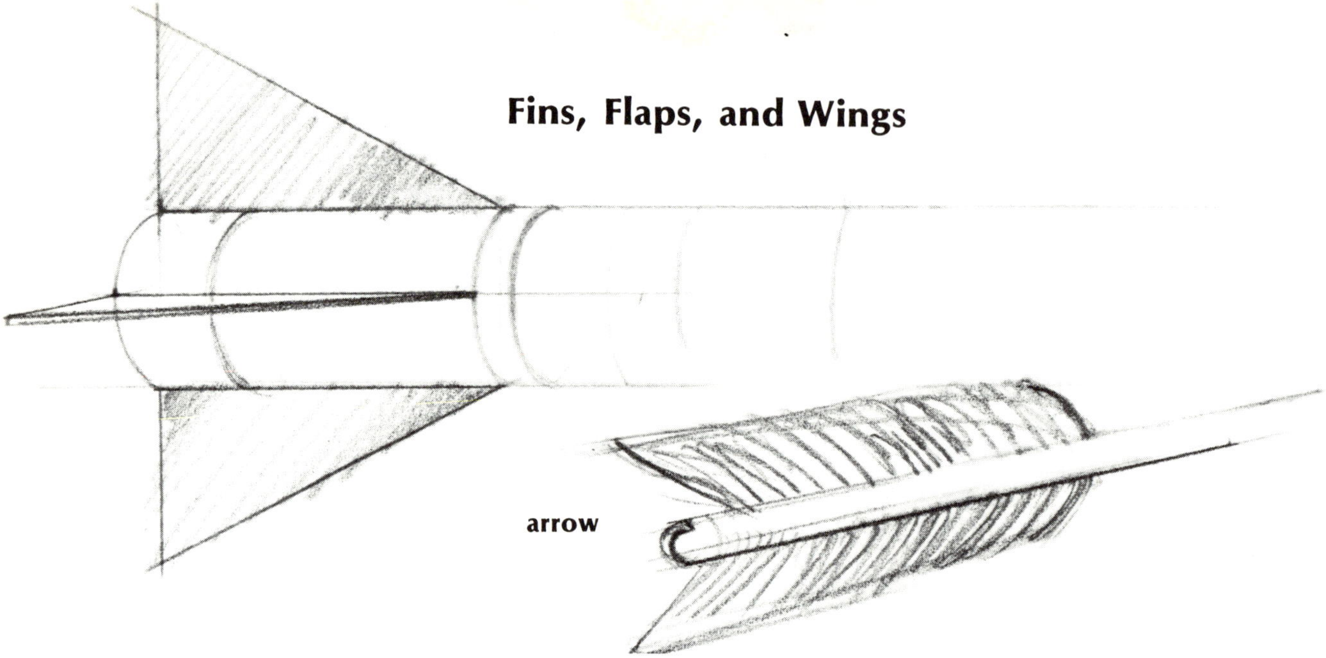

arrow

There is one more basic shape that is usually on spacecraft that operate in an atmosphere. Its shape is flat and triangular. On early rockets it was called a fin and stabilized the rocket's flight—it works much the same as feathers on an arrow.

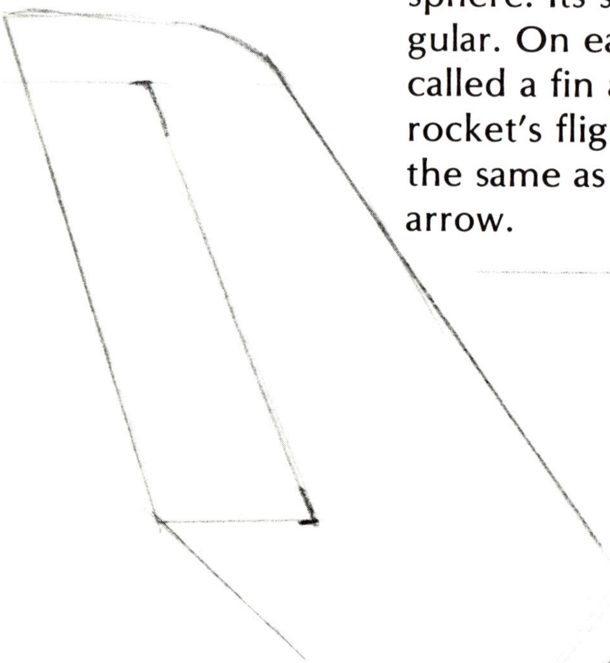

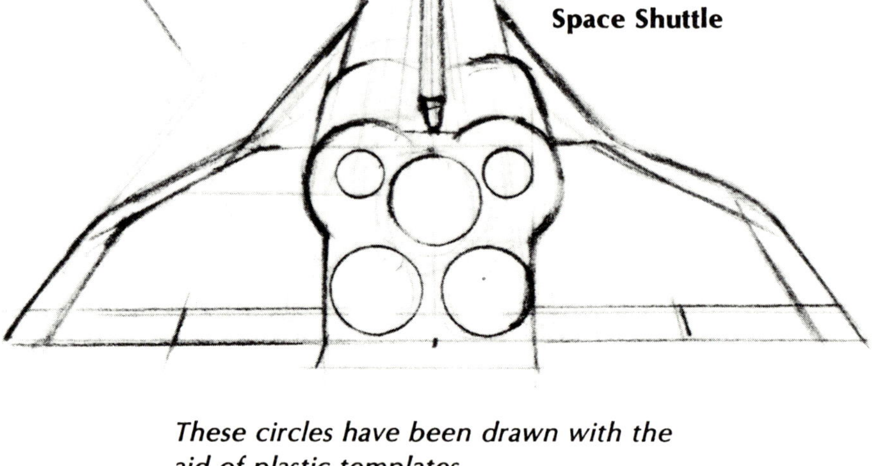

rear view of Space Shuttle

These circles have been drawn with the aid of plastic templates.

On the Space Shuttle this basic shape becomes both tail and wings. The flaps are usually on their trailing edges. These control turning (tail and wings) and up and down (tail's horizontal stabilizer). They also affect speed by increasing air resistance while landing.

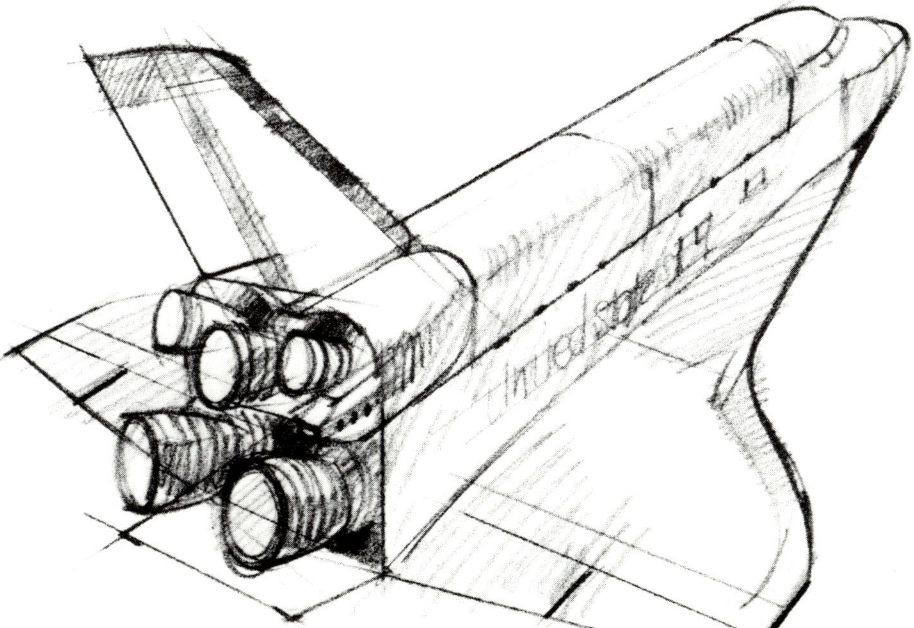

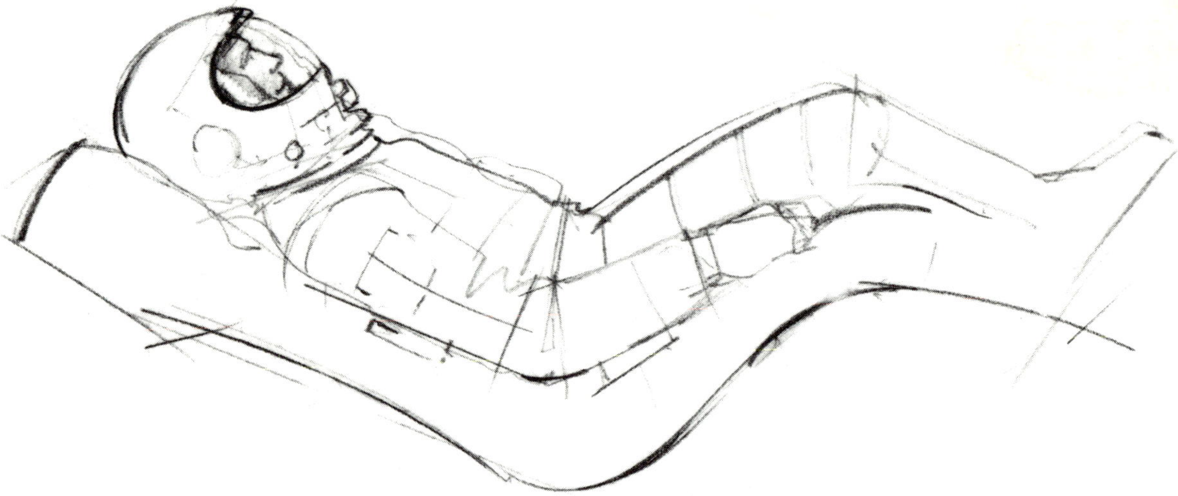

Now we know what design a spacecraft needs to blast off into space and, as in the case of the Space Shuttle, return to earth. But what about the pilots of these craft? What are the requirements for their safety and comfort? To begin with, a pilot (or passenger) requires a seat to absorb the force of lift-off. And the pilot and copilot must also be in a position to see and manipulate all the instruments on the control panel.

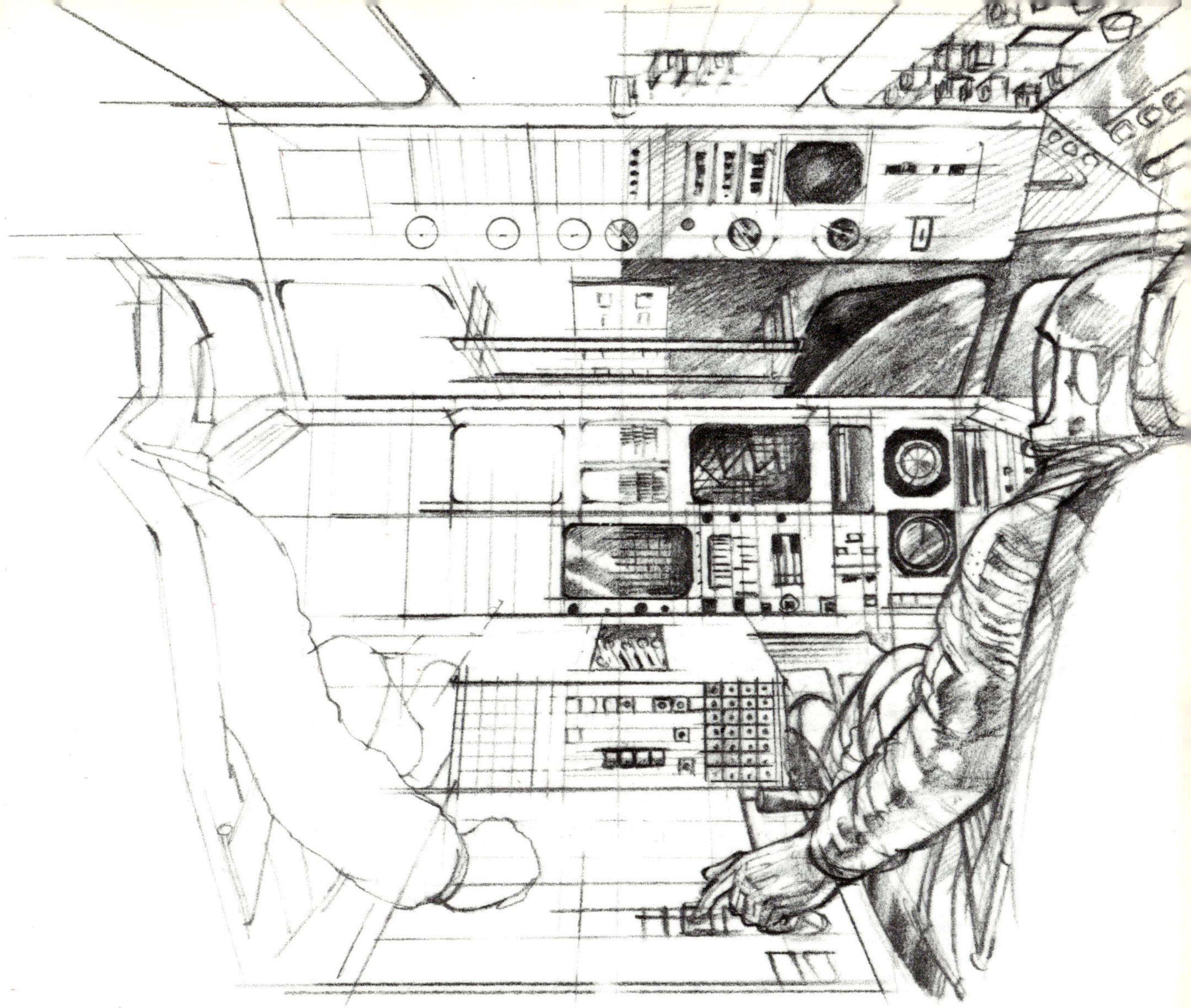

These complicated control panels are easier to draw than you might think. Use a ruler to create the basic shapes on the left. Then darken some panels (TV screens) and add some shading and highlights.

The acceleration phase is at left, and on this page the pilots are guiding the Space Shuttle into its orbit around earth.

CHAPTER 3 **In Orbit**

Here you are—out in space.

The Space Shuttle *Columbia* is in orbit around earth. It has just opened its cargo doors. Soon a space satellite will be lifted out of the shuttle. This satellite will orbit the earth just like the Space Shuttle—but unlike the Space Shuttle it will not return to earth. Satellites like it will go on orbiting the earth even after they are no longer needed or usable. These spacecraft are both different from and similar to the ones we have just drawn. They are different because they encounter no air resistance. Therefore, the bulletlike, cone-shaped fronts are not necessary; nor are wings or tails. But they do need engines to move them through space. They also need fuel for those engines. How are these needs provided? And how do they affect the shape of these spacecraft? This chapter shows some of the solutions in use. It also illustrates some future answers to the challenge of travel in space.

These small satellite spacecraft illustrate a point stressed in Chapter 2. They have basically simple shapes. Do they remind you of anything you've seen? One looks like a tin can—another like a ball. When you begin working, look first at these common objects. After that, refer to your space picture collection for details, colour, and markings.

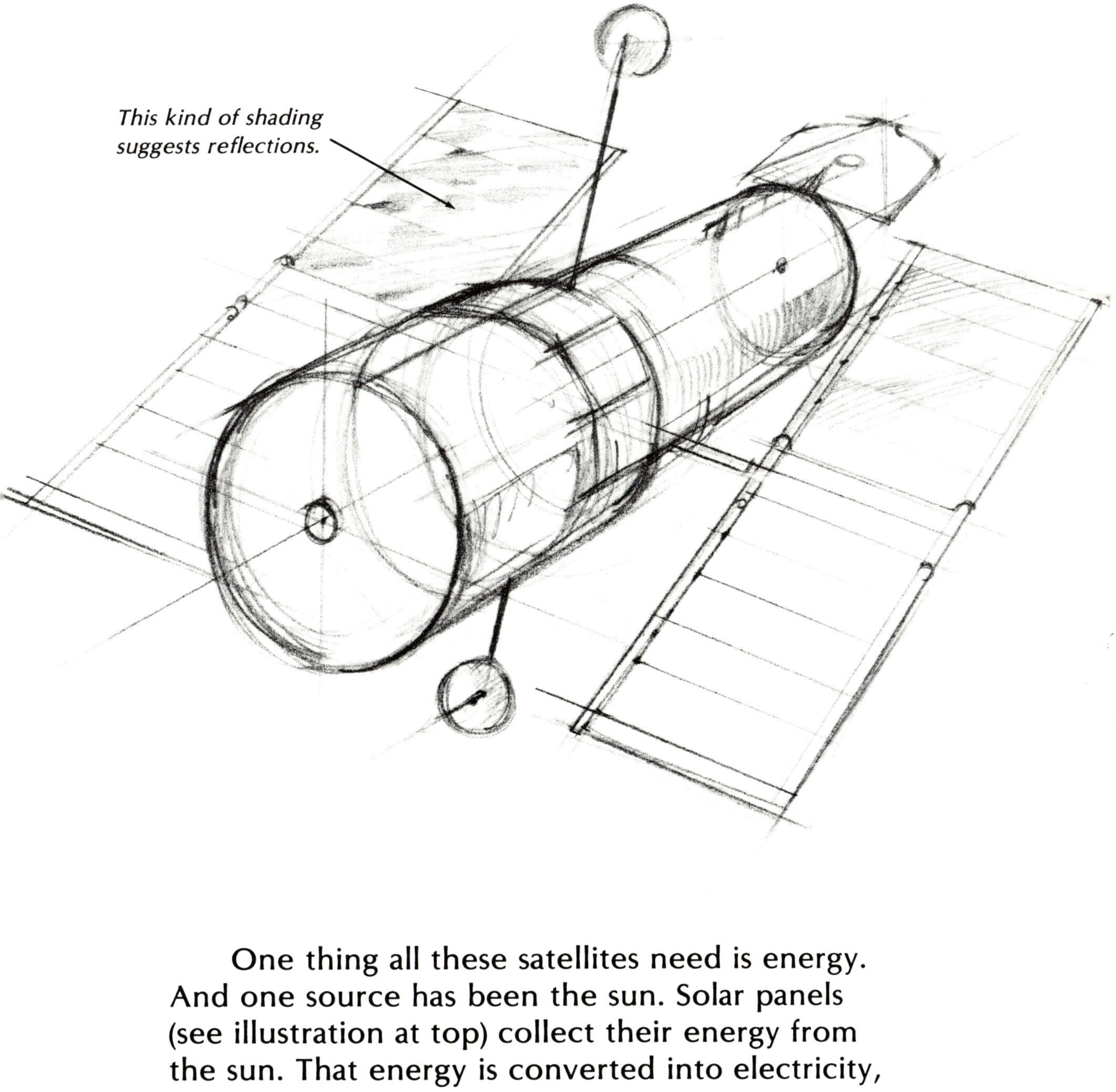

One thing all these satellites need is energy. And one source has been the sun. Solar panels (see illustration at top) collect their energy from the sun. That energy is converted into electricity, which powers all the instruments and computers.

Space Lab

The first big step in beginning a permanent colony in orbit is the Space Lab.

Again start with simple shapes. Make sure the perspective (where necessary) appears correct.

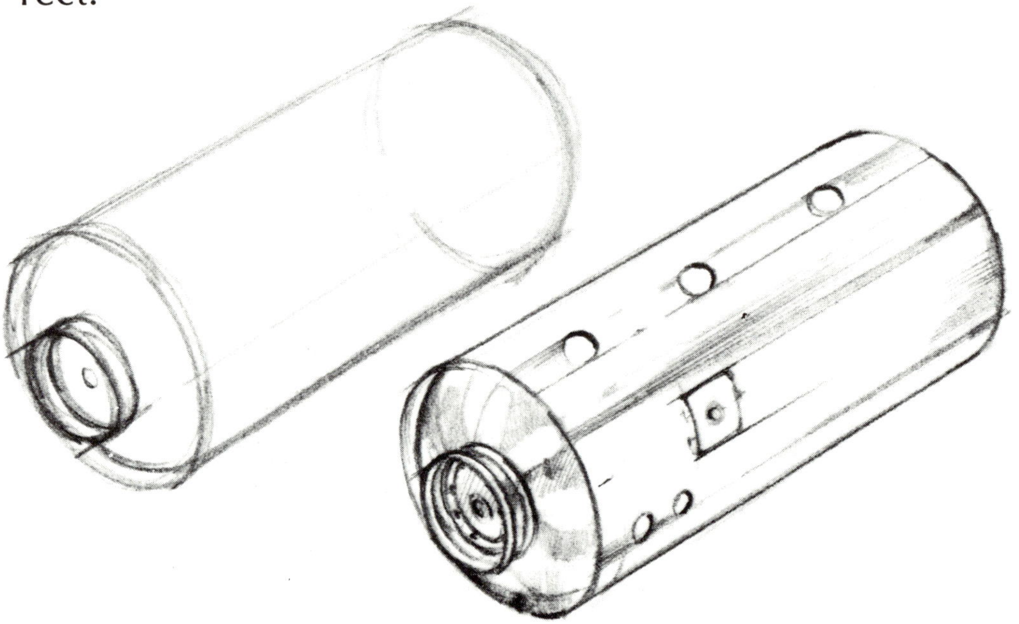

Notice that each drawing develops from a basic geometric shape into a representation of the actual satellite. Also note that the drawing at the right becomes more realistic when placed against a dark, spacelike background. (The star effect is obtained by painting white dots. Use a fine, pointed brush.)

Note the direction of the light. In space, near the sun and earth, the sunlight is intense, which means that shadows are very dark and defined.

A felt-tipped pen was used to create the dark background.

This proposed orbiting space station, a huge rotating wheel with spokes, looks very much like a bicycle wheel. And that is exactly what you can use for your first sketches.

In your beginning drawings, position the space station. See how perspective affects the spokes. Notice that the section of tube closer to you is larger.

After your sketches reach a certain point of completion, use some of the draughtsman's tools. For example, the curve will help you get a smooth contour on the tube. A ruler will make the spokes more precise.

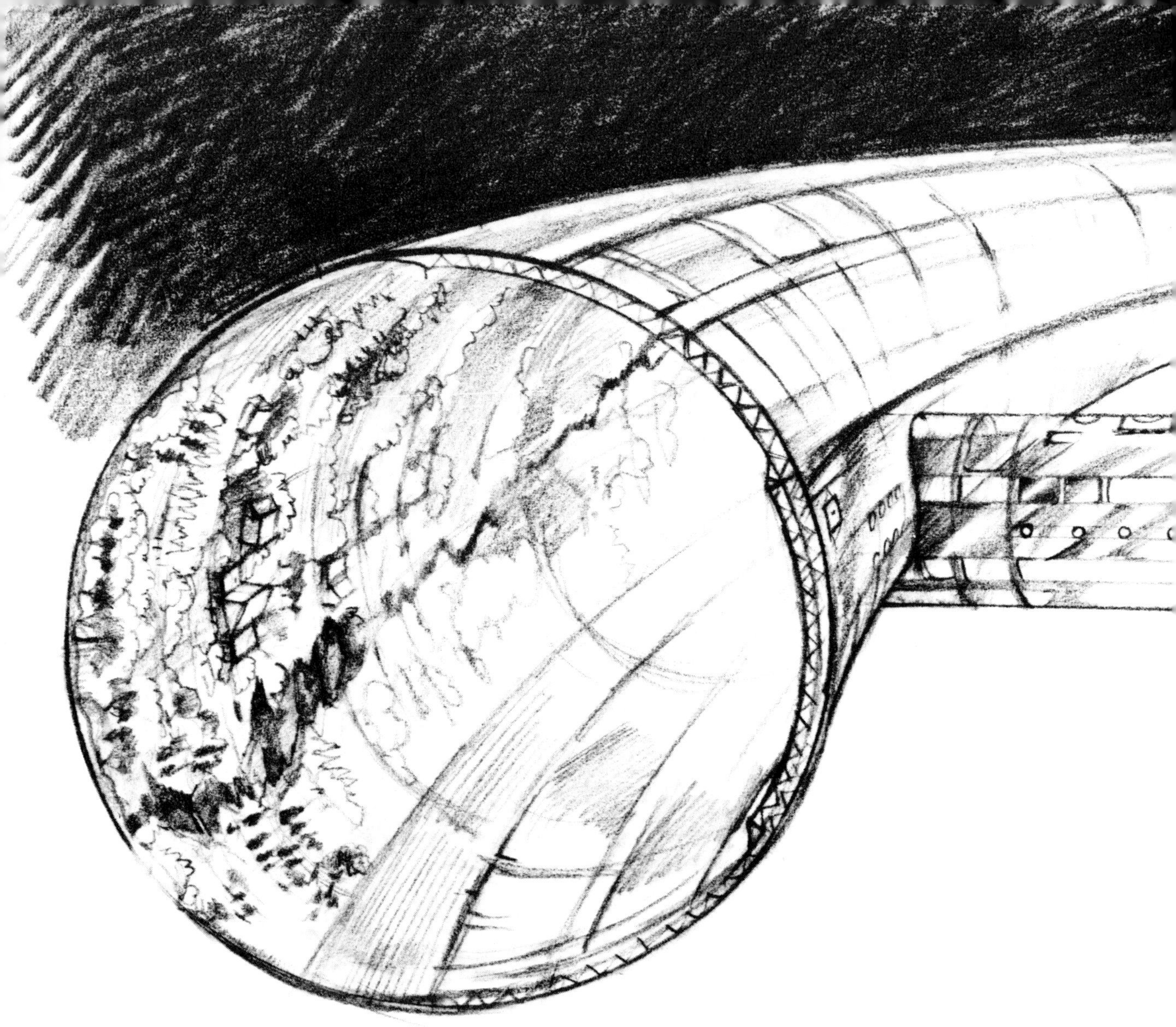

This is a cutaway view of the inside of the outer tube shown on the preceding page. The rotating wheel produces a gravity effect on the inside of its outer surface. This means that an earthlike existence is possible—complete with landscape, houses, water, earthlike gravity, etc.

Note how the living surface curves "upward" in both directions from any one point.

Another space station design is the rotation tube. Each tube is about 219 yards (200 m) across. Like the rotating wheel, its rotation produces gravity at the outer circumference.

The large panels are solar reflectors. These are lowered or raised to control the amount of sunlight to the interior of the tube.

side view

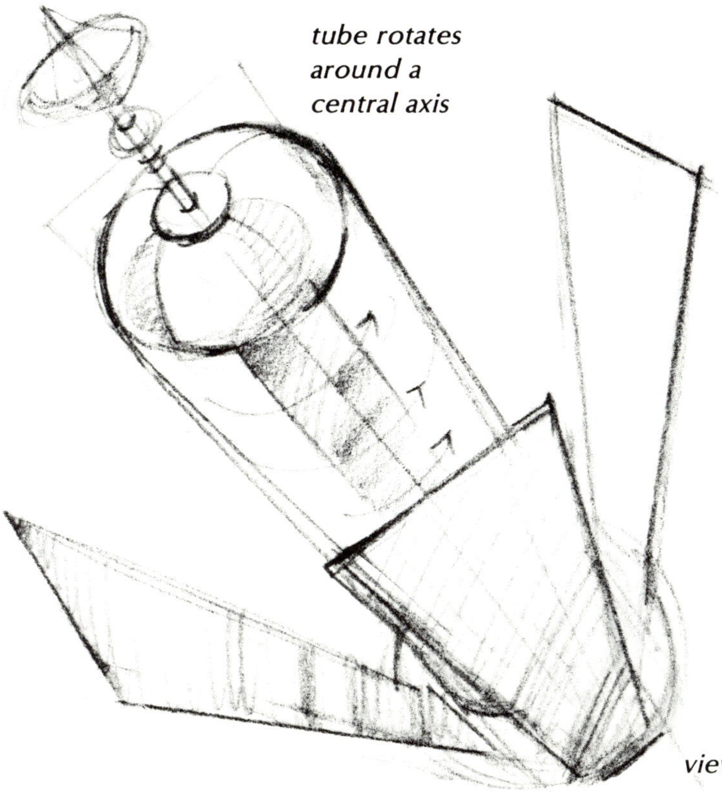

view from above

space tug

Here is the space station. A space shuttle is arriving from earth with a cargo of passengers and supplies. In this picture the different objects begin to convey a sense of outer space.

The colony is surrounded by various spaceships. These spacecraft could be the ordinary working vehicles of the future. A tug ferries materials back and forth between space colonies, while an engineering capsule oversees construction of large solar collecting platforms.

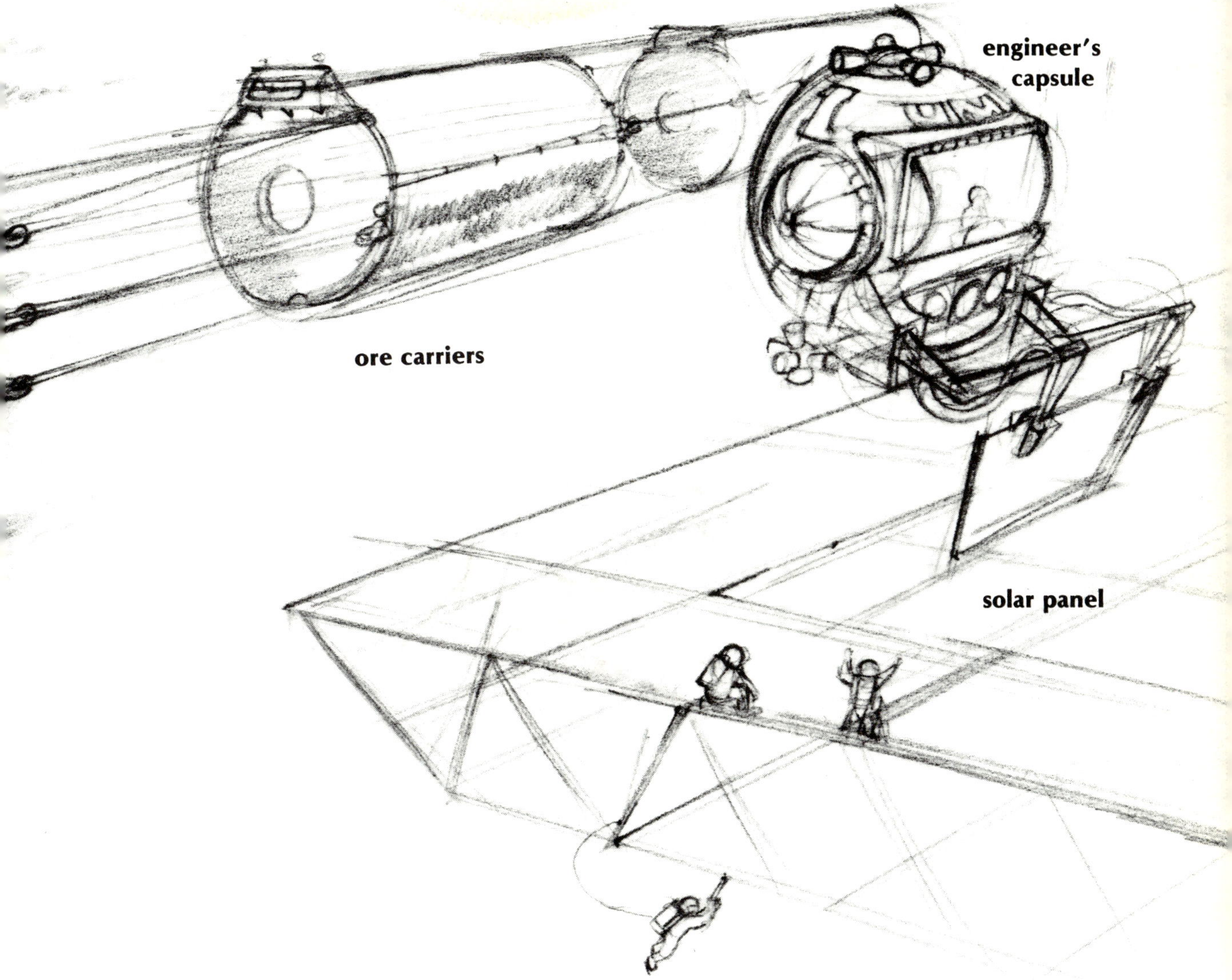

By the time that space colonies are common, many new types of spacecraft will have been invented. You can invent and design your own. Begin by imagining what job has to be done—and design a shape that would do it best.

CHAPTER 4 On to the Stars

Someday humans may explore distant space in giant spaceships. These ships would be like a complete city, equipped to care for hundreds, perhaps thousands, of people. Even with more powerful engines it would take many years to travel to the nearest star system. People on these voyages would spend their entire lives without leaving the star ship.

In this chapter we explore these ideas and see what kinds of spacecraft and equipment might be needed for this journey.

Here is one idea for a large explorer ship. Note that it is composed of many familiar shapes.

Notice that the huge rockets have basically the same design as earlier engines. The perspective and placement on the page emphasize the size of the spaceship and add a bit of drama.

As you look down on *Wanderer I*, the earth's first explorer ship, notice how the different sections suggest different uses. The huge rockets connect to the power sections. The two smaller domes, top and bottom, seem to be observatories. The largest dome is the main living and working area.

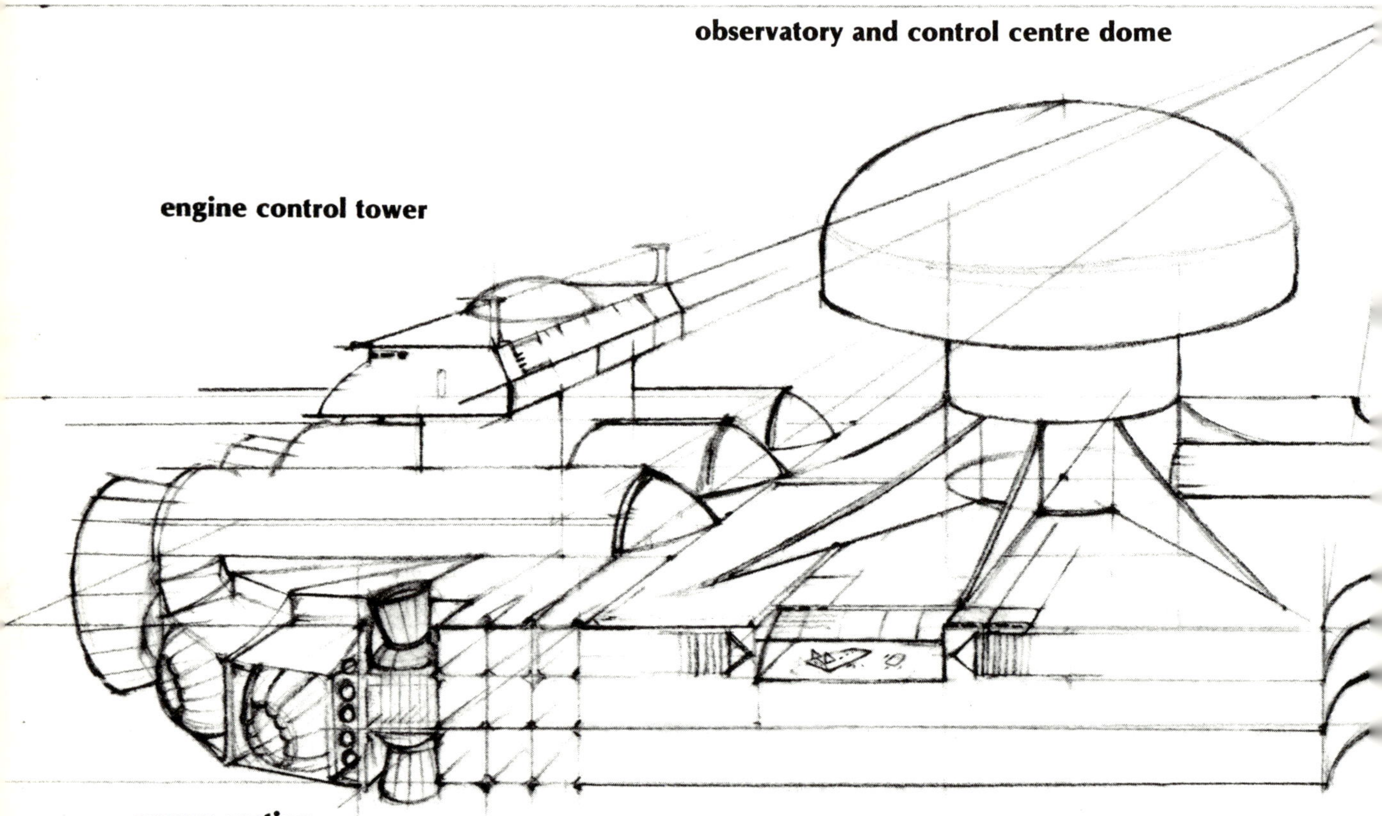

When drawing such large and seemingly complex structures, you can use perspective to make the job simpler. In this drawing, perspective helped in drawing the hangar and power sections. After the rough, freehand sketches were made, a ruler and French curve were used to make the drawing more precise.

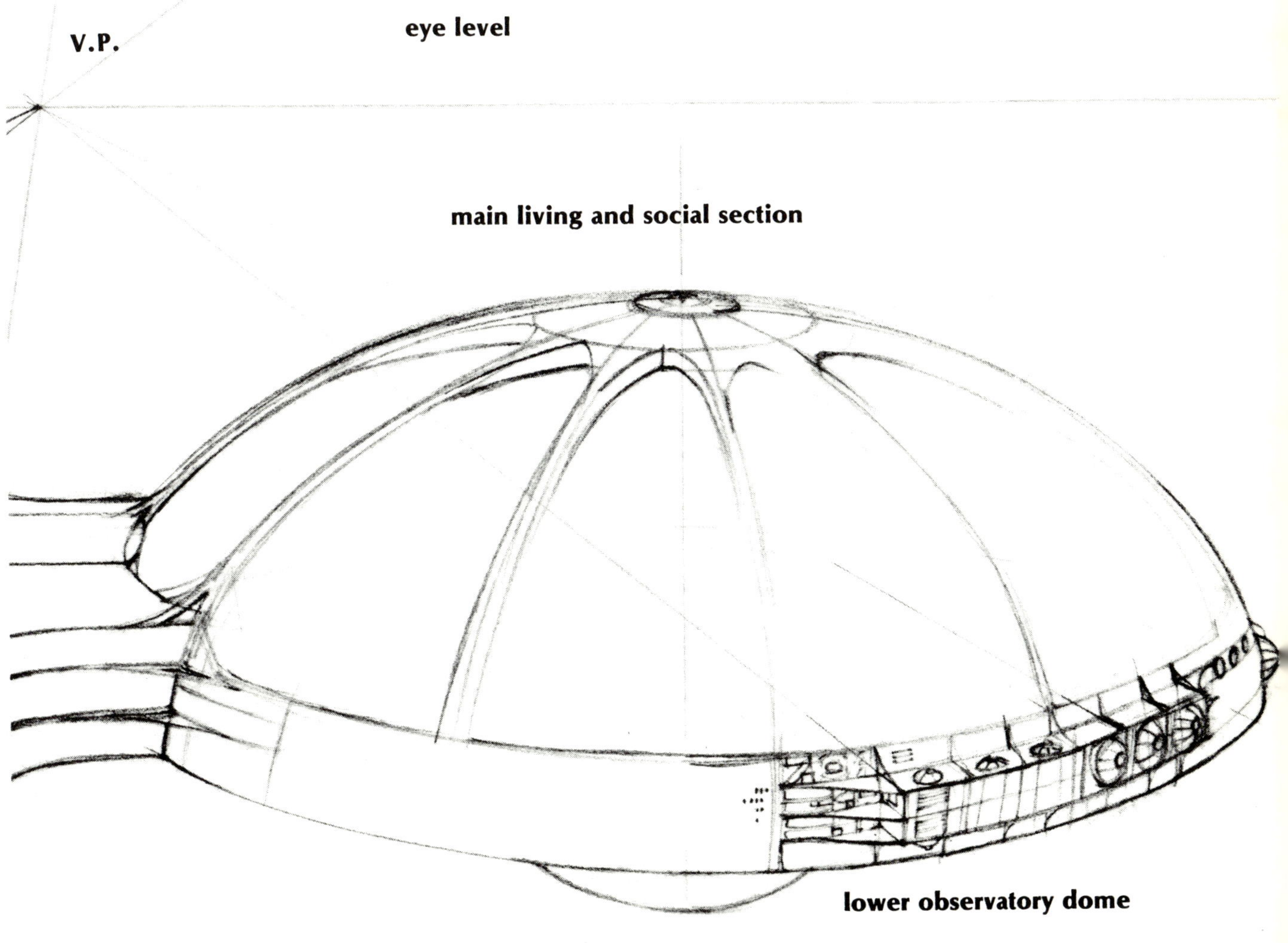

After you have drawn your spaceship in pencil line (as on the preceding pages), try a few experiments in shading. Take a piece of tracing paper, put it over your pencil drawing, and add some shadows. Keep in mind that the light source (a sun, for example) would come from one direction. In the picture below, the light source is above and to the right of the starship. Of

course, you can put your light anywhere you wish. If you have a model spaceship, put it under intense light and see how the shadows fall.

By using tracing paper over your line drawing, you can also see how different combinations of forms would look. On this drawing, for example, try changing the height of the control centre dome.

As you move closer to the giant ship, the details become clearer. Familiar shapes and textures come into view—metal plates, welded seams, tubing, identifying numerals and lettering, small platforms for repairs and service, windows, hatches, access panels. This creates a sense of scale and authenticity. Many of these details are already in use on today's spacecraft. Look closely at your picture collection for guidance when drawing the surface of your spaceship.

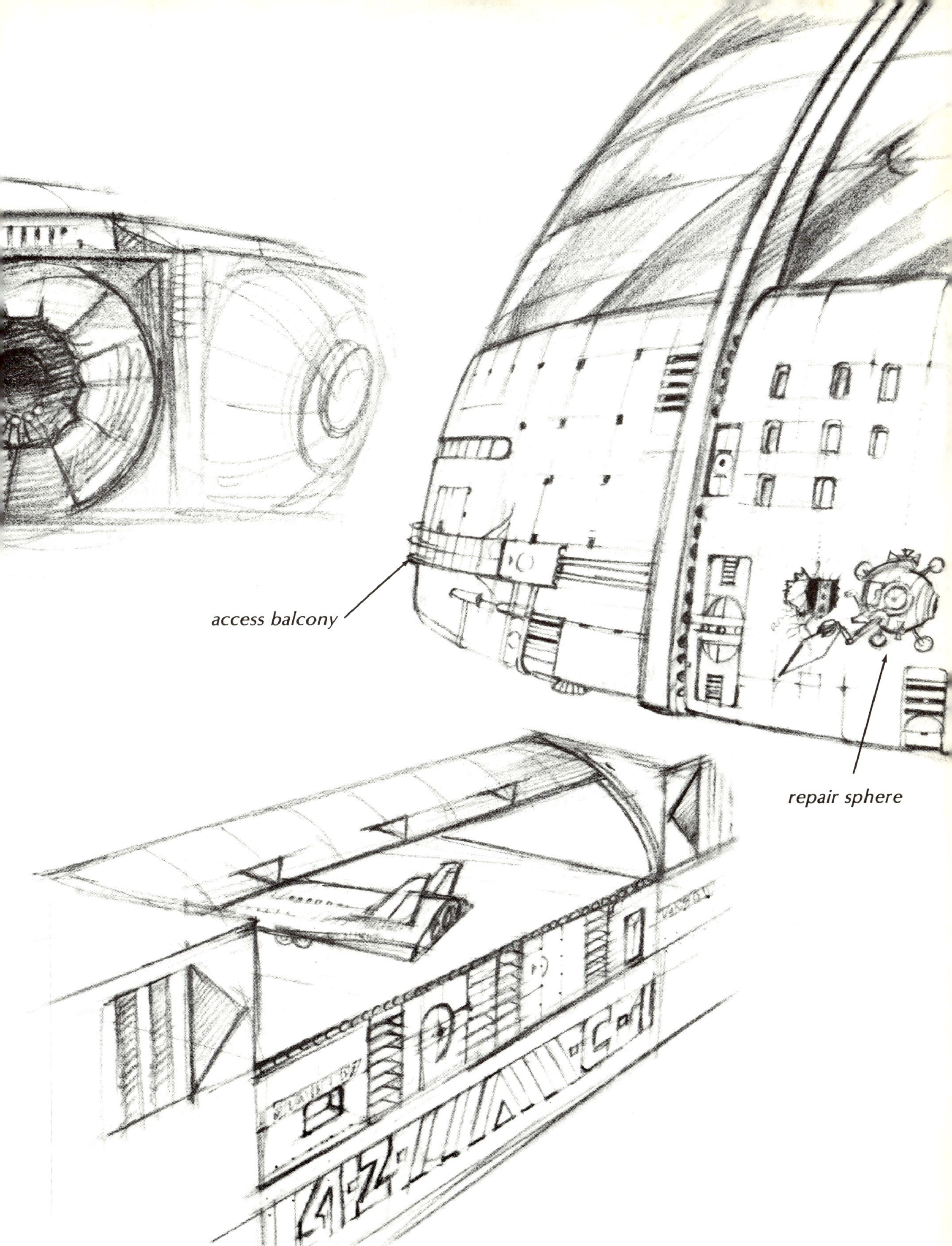
access balcony
repair sphere

You are in the main ship. Your first stop is the control room—the nerve centre and command post for the entire expedition. You might also find a section where people at a certain age would be placed in suspended animation. In this way they could survive a voyage that would take longer than an ordinary lifetime.

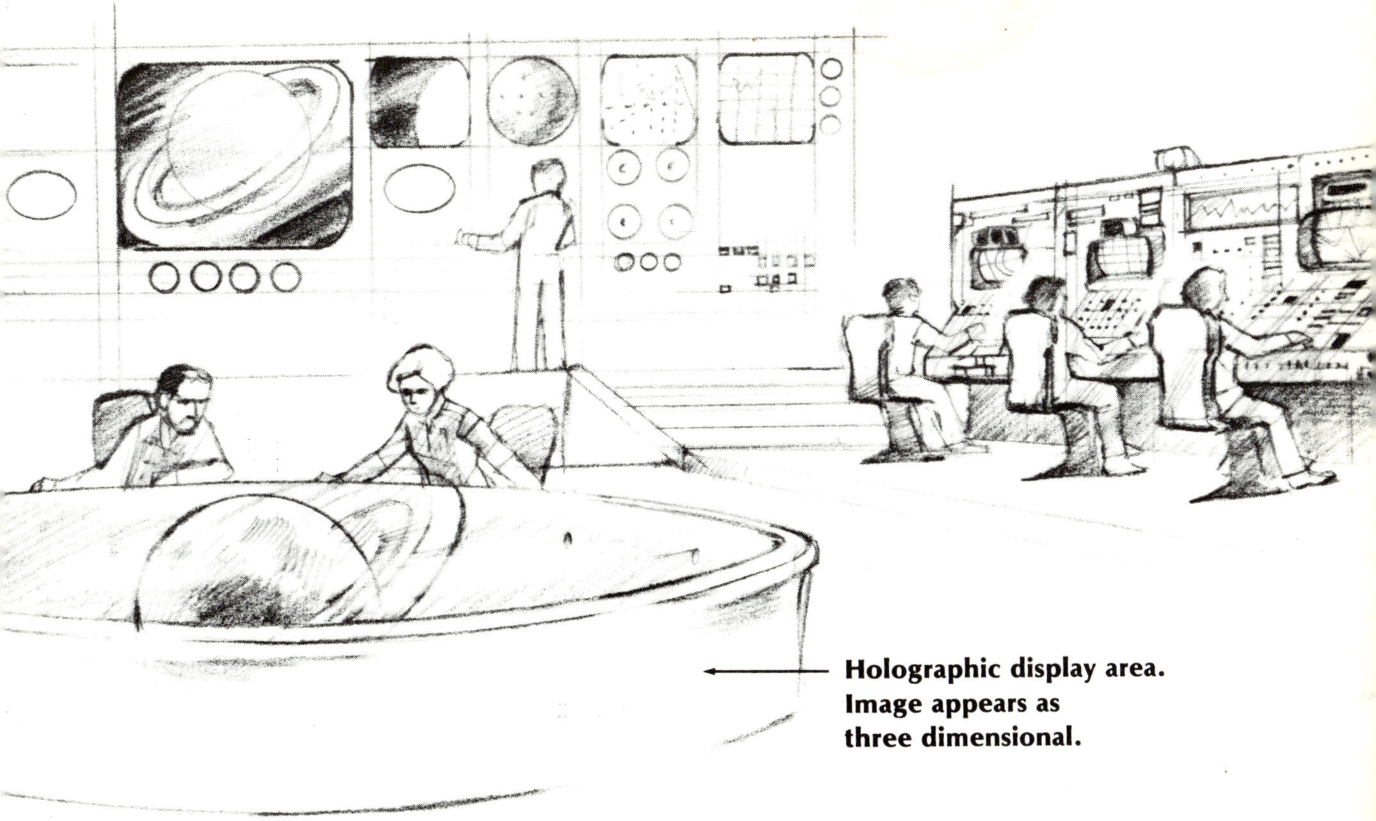

In another section is the hydroponic botanical lab. Plants here grow bigger and faster and are more nutritious than on earth.

Note how perspective creates an illusion of space.

The hangar deck is at the bottom of the middle section. It houses the auxiliary fleet of spacecraft. The defence fighters are armed with laser weapons to blast their way through an asteroid belt. Large transport cruisers stand ready if they are needed to land on a strange planet.

A small reconnaissance craft is being prepared to enter the air lock. It is about to explore a nearby asteroid for its value to the expedition.

reconnaissance craft

These drawings were done freehand,
but a ruler was used to check perspective.

DSOA-4

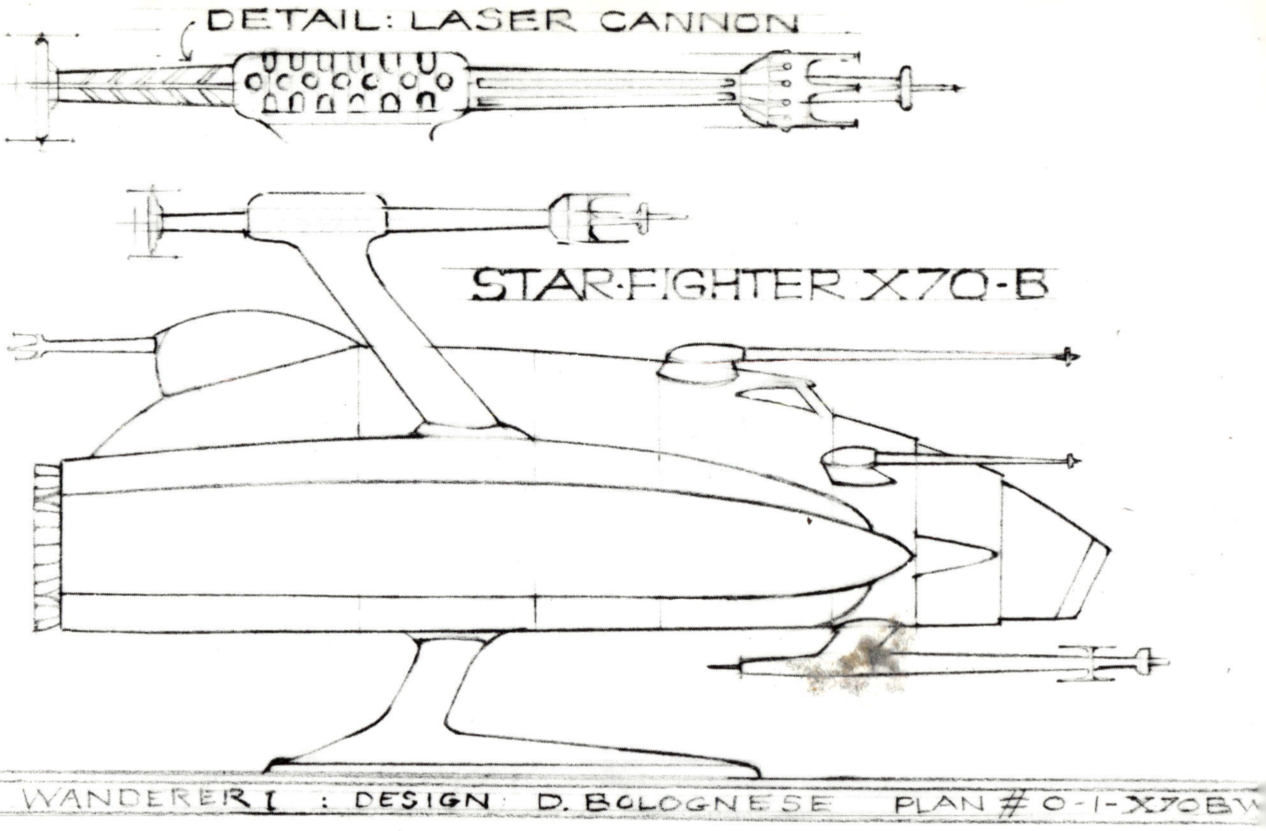

Detailed drawings—front and side view—show armaments and other external gadgets. You can redesign these by changing a part here and there or do one completely your own. Don't forget to look at all your favourite space pictures for inspiration.

These two blueprint-type drawings were done with rulers, French curves, and circle templates.

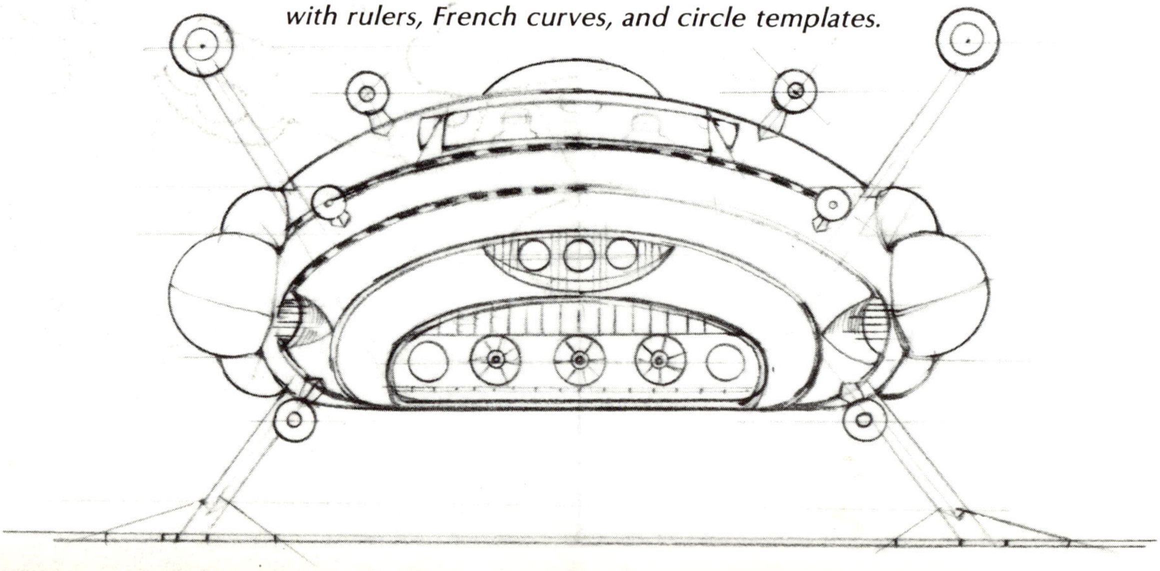

rough sketch to establish position and perspective

Notice how extreme perspective makes the fighter look as if it is going very fast.

An added moon or asteroid intensifies the sense of being in outer space.

Note sketchy circular strokes used as guide lines. These can be erased before adding finishing touches.

Bad luck! This space fighter has been struck by a laser blast from an unknown spacecraft. Instantly the pilot is ejected from the craft in an airtight cockpit. The cocoon has small rocket thrusters. They will power the small space "life raft" and make rescue easier.

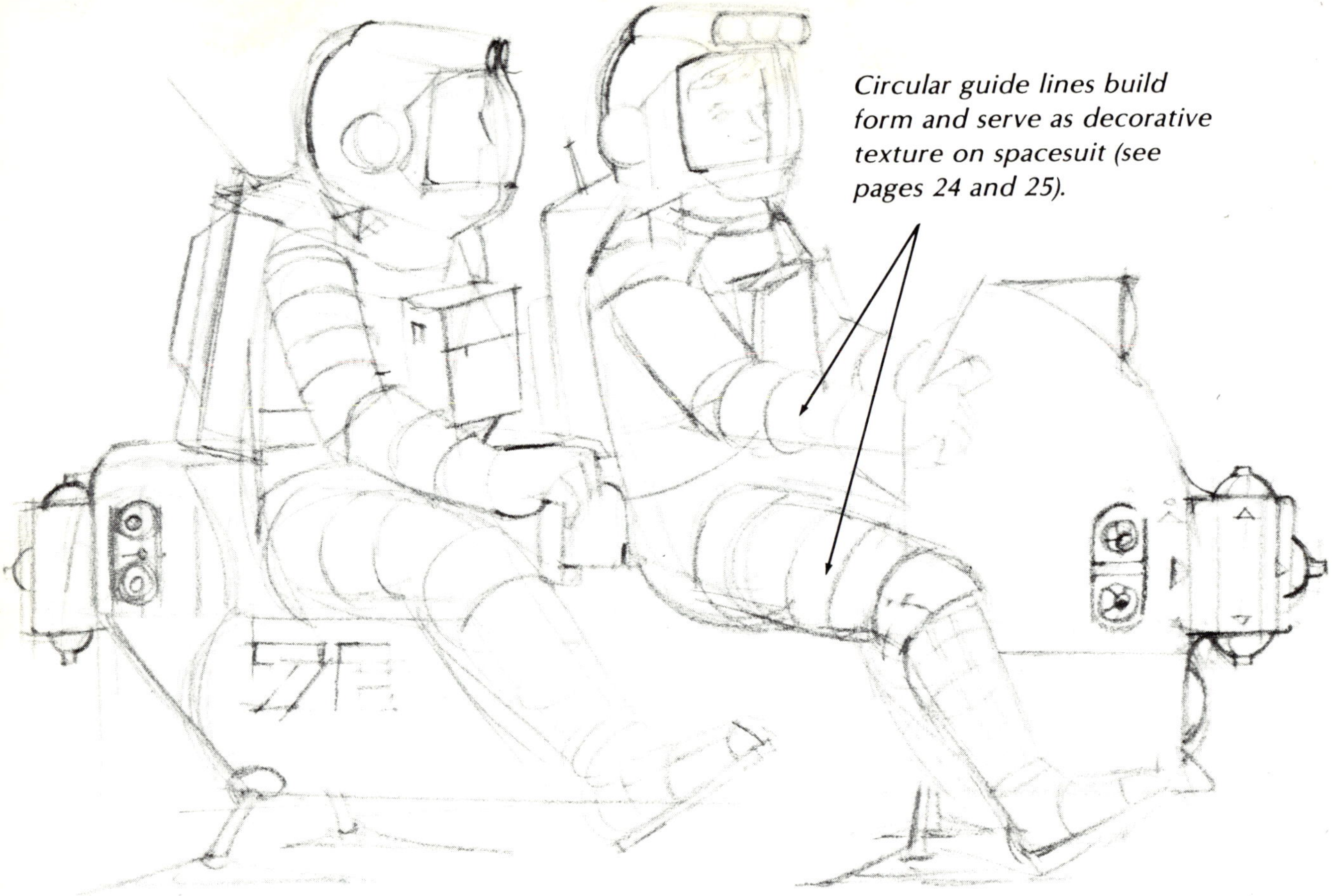

There are other small craft as well, for example, the two-seat space-scooter for repair crews.

Note small manoeuvring rockets placed at various points on the machine.

Note use of shading and erased highlights to suggest reflections.

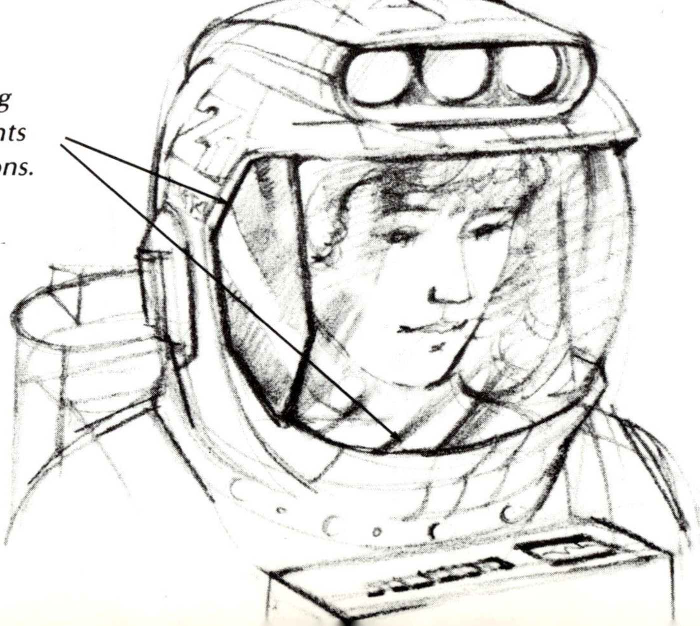

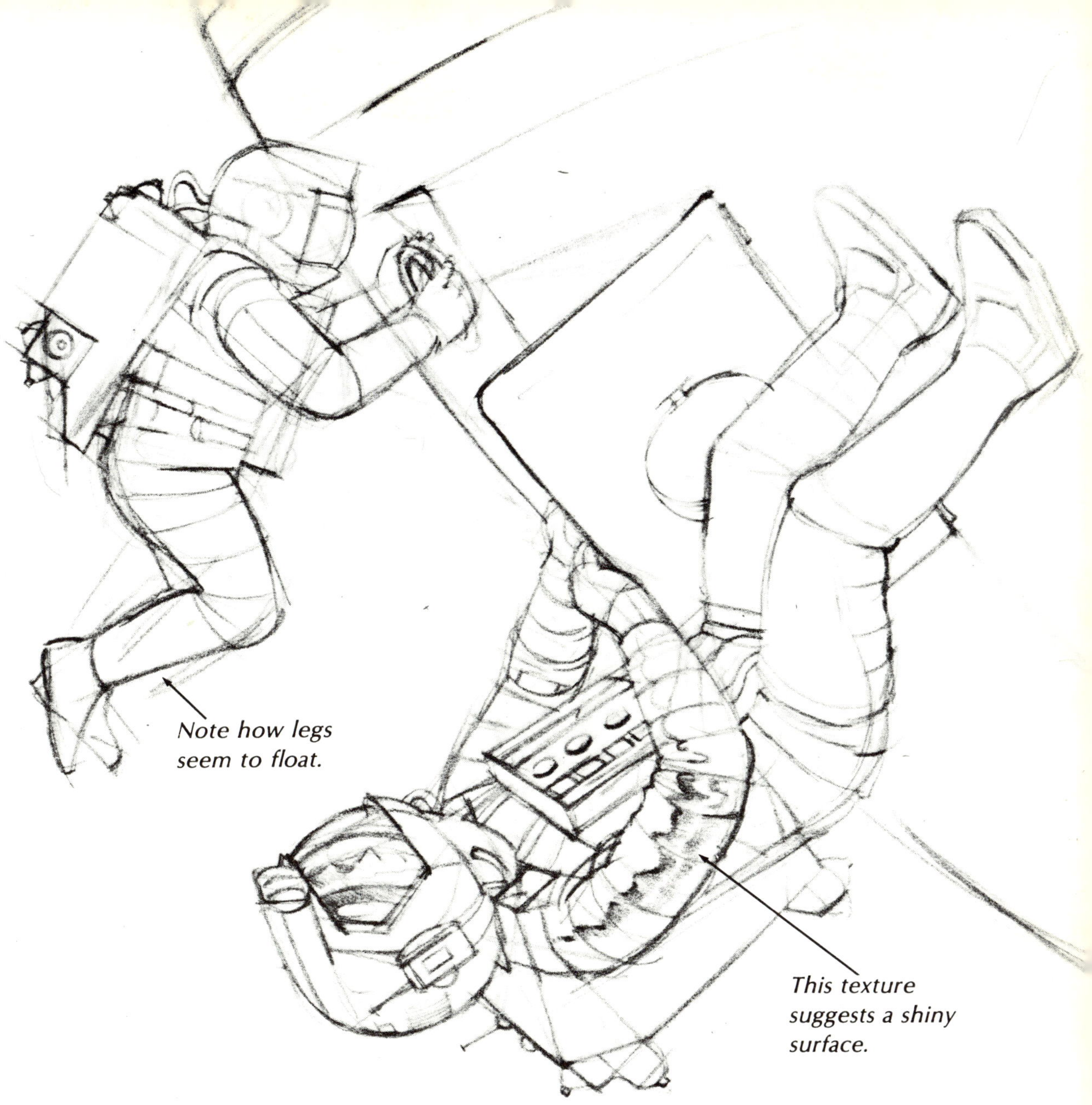

There is also a small power pack for individual travel.

Remember, because objects in space are weightless, there is no up or down. That is why this crew member must use magnetic boots to walk on the spaceship.

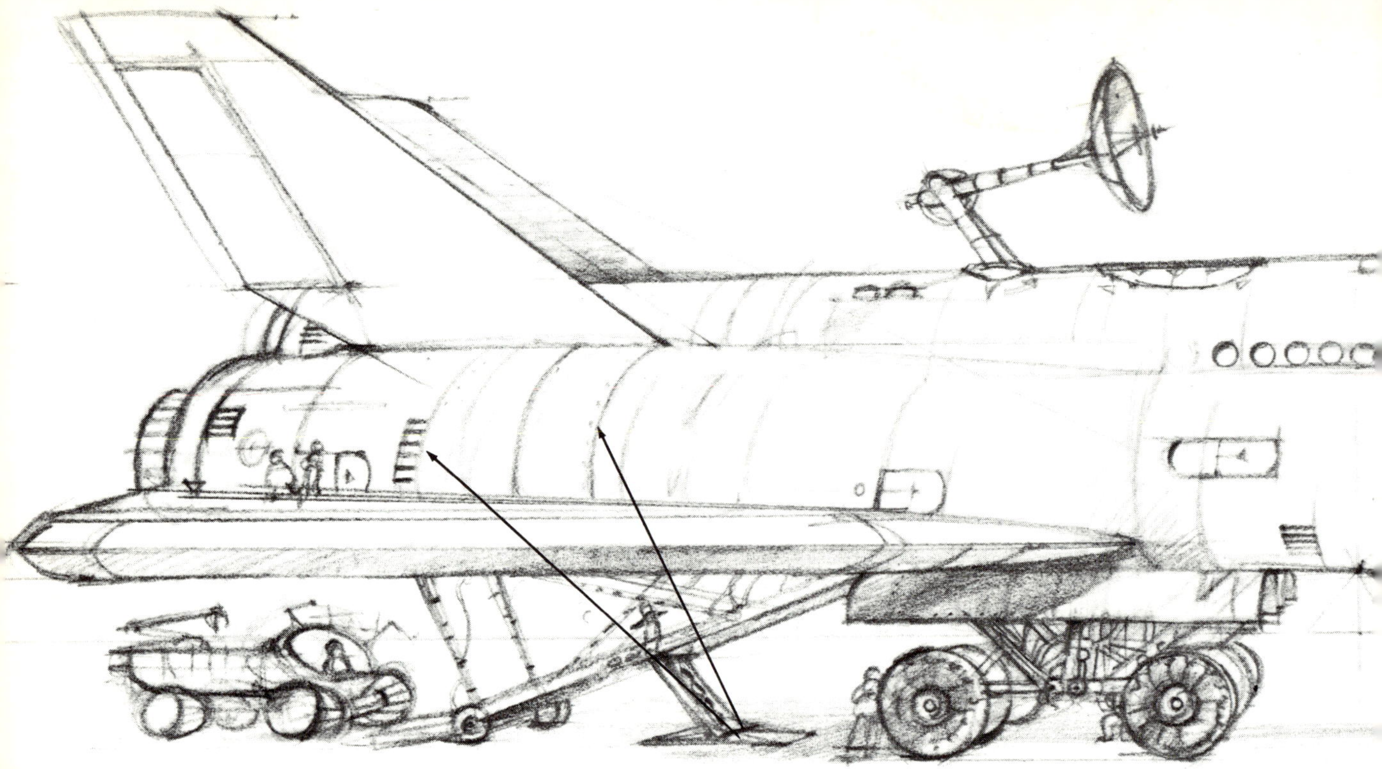

Wheeled land vehicle

Surface details should follow the contour of the form.

Fantastic news! A planet has been discovered. It has an atmosphere with oxygen and many other similarities to earth—the homeland of the space voyagers. A space cruiser is loading an exploration crew. This craft is similar to the Space Shuttle. It has retractable wings for manoeuvring in air and a smooth, streamlined shape.

On the side, a squadron of fighters is ready. They will escort the cruiser to the outer edges of the planet's atmosphere.

Note how perspective aids the drawing of rear panel on starfighter. →

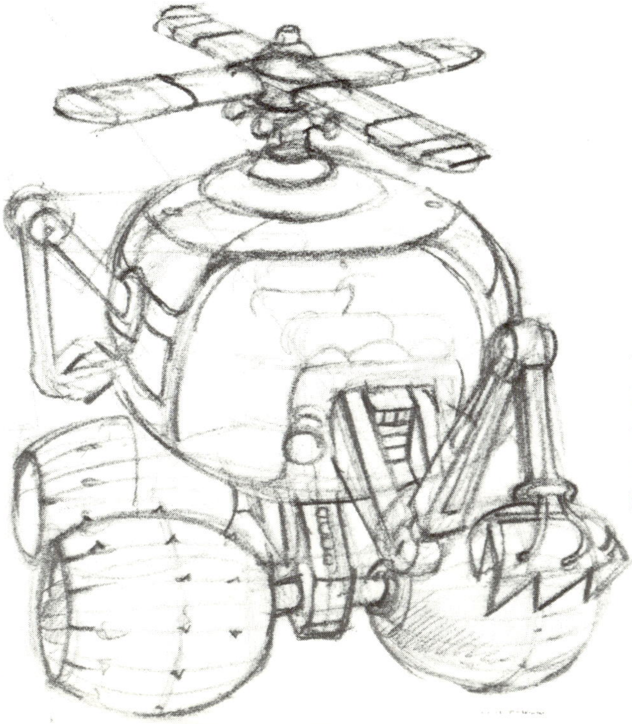

This copter-dozer (left) has telescoping rotor blades for use on planets with atmosphere. It can do its work in rugged, inaccessible areas.

The flagship hovers in orbit around the planet. The hangar doors slide open and the expedition begins its journey to the new planet.

You look out of the cockpit window at the strange planet. If all goes well with the exploration team you will be in the next landing party.

Use eraser to get the effect of rocket exhaust.
Note that the light source is above the flagship. As the space cruiser moves toward the planet, its nose comes out of the shadow of the flagship and into the light.